Pentecost Now
Pentecost Then

*A Fresh Look at the Person and Work of the
Holy Spirit today.*

Peter Butt

DEDICATION

This book is dedicated to the many spiritual fathers who have
influenced and impacted my life over the past 50 years.
This book is the result of their passion which touched my life
for the work of the Holy Spirit.
I must also thank my amazing wife, Irene who for the last 20
years has been encouraging me, challenging me and generally
provoking me to write!

CONTENTS

FOREWORDS AND COMMENDATIONS

Billy Kennedy - Leader, Pioneer network and Senior Leader, New Community Church, Southampton

'Peter's book, 'Pentecost now and then', comes from a deep conviction of the power and importance of the life of the Holy Spirit in the lives of individuals and churches today. Peter has over 40 years of church leadership experience and here he shares both his personal journey and clear theological foundations that will inspire and equip us all to reach for more.'.

John Noble - Chairman of the National Charismatic and Pentecostal Leadership Conference from 1984 – 2006

Peter Butt has always been a seeker after a deeper understanding of God's word and he also has a passion to pass on what he has learned in order to 'equip the saints for the work of ministry.' It was, therefore, almost inevitable that the Holy Spirit would lead him to put what he had learned into a form of teaching which could be used almost anywhere in the world where he travelled in ministry. His primary aim was to raise up and support mature leaders who would nurture the church and encourage the saints to reach out to fulfil the great commission to make disciples of all nations. This book on the work and person of the Holy Spirit is simply a natural progression from what has already taken place in Peter's sphere of influence. Having been around since the early days of the renewal he has seen how many leaders have taken it for granted that this new generation of Christians have received and understood what the Holy Spirit is about. When, in fact, the reality is that many New and, so-called, Charismatic churches have neglected to teach on, and more importantly, to impart the Holy Spirit to ensure that today's saints are fully immersed in the power, the presence and the practice of life in the Spirit. This book will help to get us back on track as it outlines the basic biblical essentials of understanding the work of the Spirit and encourages us to continue in positive encounters with the Spirit as we move on with God. It will also ensure that we do not lose the ground which has been wonderfully recovered through all that the Lord has done in the past 100 plus years of Pentecostal and Charismatic Renewal.

Basil D'Souza - Leader of International Christian Leadership Network and Covenant Blessings Church, Mumbai, India.

The Holy Spirit is often misunderstood and hence grieved or quenched. Peter in his book unravels some of the mystery; bringing us fresh, readable and practical insights; leading us to hunger for more, thereby encountering His presence. Having had the privilege of travelling with Peter to many cities and nations, this book is full of great memories and first hand experiences. For me it was a reliving of timeless moments when the Lord stepped in with His presence, power, anointing and grace. Peter invites us all into a growing relationship and friendship with Holy Spirit and to seek out adventure on the high seas with Him.

Come dive in!!!

E. Wayne Drain - Founding Senior Pastor - Fellowship of Christians - Arkansas, U. S.A.

"Peter Butt is a man of the spirit and a man of understanding. After serving in ministry for 40+ years he understands that any effectiveness a believer may have doesn't come by human strength or intelligence alone, but by the Holy Spirit. Peter's Pentecostal background is honored, but he has broadened his appeal to many tribes within the Body of Christ in becoming a trusted father in the faith to a new generation. This book will help you practically apply principles of living a Spirit empowered life. Read it! Then read it again!"

Paul Randerson; – Senior Pastor, Kings Lynn and Breckland Christian Fellowships:

Very easy read, loved it. You are very clear as to your position. There is good classical Pentecostal stuff and yet acknowledging the charismatic era as a move forward for the church. Your teaching on the gifts and tongues and going East is great particularly in application.

It is very honest I can see it appealing to the younger generation as you have such a breadth of experience. It is very sound doctrinally and contains some great stories of your travels which pull you in. I think it will be a good read and a reference book to leaders. Well done!

Sylvia Weir – Kings Church, Barking:

I think this is a brilliant book and your heart to see people come into a deeper experience of the Holy Spirit comes through clearly. I pray that many will be challenged and inspired to know Him more through what they read.

INTRODUCTION:
WHY I WROTE THIS BOOK AND
WHY YOU NEED TO READ IT!

Another book on the Holy Spirit.

Do we not have enough? These would be reasonable comments and I would have some sympathy with them except for one thing. I am writing this book because I believe I have been encouraged by the Holy Spirit to write it.

I have been in church leadership and ministry for over 45 years. I pastored my first church in North London in 1970. I was part of the Pentecostal church in the UK, went through their Bible College and ministered for over 15 years as part of the movement. I then transitioned to the new church movement where my ministry has been ever since. Over those years I have seen the impartation of the Holy Spirit as a significant part of my ministry and calling. Looking back, I recognise a passion for people to have a personal encounter with the Holy Spirit.

Before exploring this subject I would like to share with you a little of my own history. My father was a good model of an evangelical Christian. He witnessed regularly and saw several people come to the Lord as well as being a fully committed member of the church. He was fully involved in Sunday school and youth work and was a generous contributor financially. He went with his best mate, Fred, to argue with the local Pentecostal Pastor about tongues and came back speaking in languages he had never learnt. The difference in his walk with God when he was filled with the Holy Spirit was quite staggering. For the rest of his days he lived in that anointing and experience, seeing God work at a different level in his life.

As a teenager I was filled with the Holy Spirit at a Christian Holiday centre in North Wales. The instruction I received has shaped my life in the Spirit. I felt the call of God to ministry and was a student at the Assemblies of God Bible College. As students we served at their Annual General Conference and were invited to help at the "Receiving meeting", a late night gathering to encourage people to be filled with the Spirit for the first time. It was an awesome sight to see up to 500 people receiving the Baptism of the Holy Spirit in a few short hours. That inspired me, and there a desire was birthed in my heart to impart the Spirit. Over the years as I became a minister of the church I would make a point of being part of that annual event and was used by God to impart the Holy Spirit as I was inspired by John Philips and Clyde and Norman Young, well known leaders in the Pentecostal movement.

I became involved in the development of a Youth Camp work where we saw around 200 young people a week attend over the month of August each year. There would be one evening each week when we preached on the Holy Spirit and invited young people to be filled with the Spirit. We would see at least 30 young people respond and usually at least 20 would receive the Spirit each week. Sometimes we experienced a spontaneous move of the Spirit which resulted in many more receiving the Spirit. Over a period of 15 years we saw hundreds, perhaps thousands, receiving the Spirit.

Since that time it has been a part of the ministry in which God has used me; I seem to have been given a measure of faith to believe for people to receive the Spirit. There have been many individuals and some corporate times when I have seen God fill many with the Holy Spirit, speaking in tongues and encountering the presence and power of God.

One highlight of recent years was in India with the Hindi speaking congregation of a church in Mumbai. I was at the end of a busy ministry trip and after several weeks this was the last meeting on a Sunday evening. I was tired but the Pastor asked me to speak on the baptism of the Holy

Spirit. I agreed but said I would not pray for individuals but pray over the whole congregation. There were around 120 people in the building. They all stood to receive the Holy Spirit. As I prayed for the Spirit to fall upon them, around two thirds of the congregation were filled with the Spirit during a period of around 20 minutes. About 80 people immediately receiving the promise of the Father. The Pastor told me later he had sat next to a lady who arrived in the meeting and was a little drunk. They had been trying to help her and she was responding to the gospel but struggling with an alcohol problem. He was astounded as he saw her filled with the Holy Spirit and speaking fluently in the language of the Spirit.

This is a brief history of my experience of people being filled with the Holy Spirit. It is to this backdrop that I bring my contribution to the question of what it means to be "baptised in the Holy Spirit", gathered over the last 50 years.

There are two major reasons why I believe this book is necessary:

1. Prophetic encouragement.

Over the past 3 years I have been ministering on the subject of the Holy Spirit, encouraging people to expect a greater, more powerful encounter with the person of the Holy Spirit. I believe the Lord has given me prophetic insight and dreams which I have put together in a series of preaching and teaching during that time. This makes up Part 1. of the book.

About 18 months into this period of time at the Pioneer Leaders' Conference in March 2015 we held a small gathering of leaders from a number of nations attending the conference. A leader from the USA called Wayne Drain was given opportunity to share prophetically. He did not know anything about me apart from my name. This is the word he spoke personally to me:

"It is not winding down, it's cranking up. Active, movement, going here-going there. That's just the season you are in. You should ride it like a good surfer rides the waves. Another season, perhaps another wave, perhaps a season on the beach with your feet up in a lounge chair. But in this season it's a time of activity, a time of movement, going here-going there. Here is your word. "Enjoy this season!" Enjoy this part of the journey. Equip, Empower, Input, Impart - This is your focus. God will give you all you need. Don't question the season you are in, just give yourself to it with joy. Another season, a book that will help many sons and daughters. You are writing the chapters now as a living Epistle. Later you will make it plain, you will write it down so that others can ride the waves in their season". (Wayne Drain. 3.5.2015.)

This word came as I was in the season of ministering on the Holy Spirit so I immediately knew what the subject of the book was to be. Just a few weeks later another prophetic ministry from North Carolina sent me the following confirmation.

"Son, I am coming at this time to strengthen your physical body. There is much work for you to do and I am coming to build up your body in every way- bones, muscles, and your immunity system.

Directives will come from the throne room and a new commissioning as one who is sent. A Father's heart I have placed within you. You will go to instruct, teach, and impart. You will set up proper boundaries for the river of outpourings to come upon My people. Like a rush of flood waters, I will flow into the lives of My people in new and fresh ways. Many will receive new baptisms, refreshing, and empowering as you minister. Also, a new anointing will open up over you to call out the secrets of the heart. Many will fall down and acknowledge that I am 'in this place' as they hear your prophecies and words of knowledge.

Irene's (my wife) gift of discerning of spirits will skyrocket at this time. She will separate soul from spirit and joints from marrow. Her ministry will be characterized by depth of insight and tremendous healing of soul and spirit. She, like a skilled surgeon, will open up My people in the Spirit. As she opens them, she will take out the bad and put in new parts. She will reach into the heavenly storehouses to retrieve new parts and insert them by faith. She will move filled with angelic fire and determination to see My Kingdom established.

She will also sort out true servants from the false. She will flow in rebuking, correcting and exhorting My people. She will fulfil her part to present a bride that is spotless and blameless. Tremendous joy will fill your own home to refresh, strengthen and encourage you both. Your best years are now!" (Paul Jobe. 23.3.15)

We were already experiencing and seeing the fulfilment of these words. They confirmed what was happening, although we are still looking for a greater release of the presence and power of the Holy Spirit.

It was then several months later during a telephone conversation that a friend of mine, who had no idea about these prophetic words, mentioned that during that morning, without any thought of me, a word had dropped in his mind that he believed was from God.

It was simply: "It is time to write the book". So here it is!

2. Greater Clarity.

The second reason for the book is the need for some basic and clear biblical foundations around the person of the Holy Spirit. As I have been ministering on the person of the Holy Spirit and issues surrounding this subject, such as the gifts of the Spirit and speaking with tongues, I have become aware of serious weaknesses in people's theology and understanding. Confusion reigns! I have felt increasingly concerned about this and so Part 2 of the book is a biblical presentation of my understanding of these matters.

I thank God for my early years of Pentecostal Theology but realise my understanding has been adjusted by years of study and experience in the wider church. I hope some of the things I recount will be of help to many as they explore the wonderful person of the Holy Spirit as revealed in the Holy Scriptures. For me the most important Biblical content is found in chapters 4-7 of Part 2 where we deal with the Baptism in the Holy Spirit. If you are looking for an encounter with the Holy Spirit please turn to these chapters.

Peter Butt, March 2017

PART ONE

PENTECOST NOW

AN ENCOURAGEMENT TO EXPECT AN
OUTPOURING OF THE HOLY SPIRIT ON
THE CHURCH IN THESE DAYS.

1

PENTECOST NOW

I was visiting Uganda and invited to speak on Pentecost Sunday at one of the congregations of the International Christian Fellowship in Kampala. It was requested that I speak on Acts 2 as part of a series they were working through as a church. My initial reaction was a very positive one as I thought I have spoken so many times on Acts 2 and read so much about this chapter that this should be a relatively easy task. I immediately felt a rebuke as the Holy Spirit seemed to say "Read the passage again carefully; I have something to show you that you have never seen before" I revisited the chapter and read again carefully, listening for the Lord to speak as I read.

This is what I saw. My first thoughts were regarding the context. The disciples were instructed to *"Wait in Jerusalem until they were clothed with power from on high". (Luke 24:49)*. Jesus, the head of the church was very clear. "You cannot build the church, reach the world, fulfil your calling, without the presence and power of the Holy Spirit". So much of our activity and programmes are initiated and organised without the sense of Holy Spirit guiding, leading and empowering and we wonder why the results are so poor. I became aware afresh of the significance of Pentecost.

Secondly as I read Acts chapter 2, I became aware of the life changing encounter that the first disciples experienced on that first outpouring of the Spirit. The marks of Pentecost were about receiving something of the supernatural life of God. They had a remarkable and powerful encounter with the person of the Holy Spirit. There was noise like a violent rushing wind; there was fire on their heads; they were filled with the Spirit speaking in languages they had never learnt. *(Acts 2:1-4)*. Such was the impact of this experience that, as they publicly began to speak in these remarkable languages, a crowd gathered and were amazed and astonished as they heard the mighty deeds of God being spoken in their own languages by simple, Galilean fisherman. *(Acts 2:5-13)*. It was clearly a remarkable supernatural occasion.

There also seemed to have been a physical response reflected in their movement because they were accused by some of being drunk. There was obviously some activity that drew that response to such a degree that Peter finds it necessary to correct their observation. *(Acts 2:13-15)*

It was then as I read the account of Peter preaching to the crowd, that I noticed something I had not seen before. I had been led to believe that we should not expect this same powerful encounter with the Holy Spirit experienced by these disciples on the day of Pentecost. These remarkable signs were apparently only for the initial outpouring of the Spirit. All the teaching I received at the Bible College, all the books I had read, all the preaching I heard over the years on this passage had suggested that we should not expect the wind and the fire or any particular supernatural encounter, but rather just be satisfied with speaking in tongues or some indication of God's presence. As I read, I felt something in me react to this idea, feeling I had been misled into not accessing all there was for me to know of a relationship with the Holy Spirit.It was as I read on that I saw that Peter clearly emphasised that the "This" they had experienced was a fulfilment both of the promise of the scripture in Joel and the promise of Jesus to them before he ascended to heaven. *(Acts 2:16, 33)*. There were no qualifying statements, no suggestions that this was a special outpouring just for them. In fact, he then goes on to say that all those from future generations should expect the same. *(Acts 2:16, 33)*. As I read, I felt the Holy Spirit say that we had accepted a watered down baptism of the Holy Spirit, accepting a mediocre experience and that He was encouraging us to raise our level of expectation on what it means to be "filled with the Holy Spirit"; that we should be looking for a greater manifestation of the miraculous and supernatural power of God to be released among us. My conviction is that God is speaking to us prophetically to believe for the Baptism of the Holy Spirit to be a significant and powerful event in our spiritual journey.

It was then an encouragement to receive a photograph and explanation from a friend of mine just a few days later with a photograph from Mozambique showing a prayer gathering where fire had appeared on the head of a number of ladies as they had been praying. It felt like a confirmation of what the Lord was saying to me; that we should be believing for the Holy Spirit to come in signs and wonders and not in a passive, mediocre way.

I was also inspired by Peter's preaching on the day of Pentecost as he explained the nature of what was occurring. He spoke of three particular things that are evidence of the work of the Holy Spirit.

1. The release of the supernatural.

Peter emphasised that the evidence of the work of the Spirit was expressed in prophecy, dreams and visions, all manifestations that require supernatural origins. *(Acts 2:16, 33)*. He declares that these things will mark the outpouring of the Holy Spirit. This encourages me as I look back over 50 years of church life. In my early days in Pentecostal gatherings very few people exercised spiritual gifts. Only one or two in most local churches ever brought prophetic words. Today in many new churches both Charismatic and Pentecostal significant numbers of believers are hearing from God and bringing prophetic words. I suggest that this a sign of increasing Holy Spirit activity.

2. Barriers down.

Peter spoke of three barriers that will be affected by the work of the Holy Spirit. Firstly, the issue of gender. It is very significant that it mentions "sons and daughters" and "servants, men and women" *(Acts 2:17,18)*. I believe we are seeing the raising up of men and women in these days. Clearly ministry will break out among the women as well as the men when the Spirit is poured out. It is not an accident or an action of militant feminism that is seeing a whole generation of women being raised up and released in ministry, but rather an evidence that the Spirit is at work. I believe there will be significant increase in an army of women raised up in these days as a prophetic sign! *(Ps. 68:11 (NASB)).*

Secondly, Peter removes the barrier of age; "old men will dream dreams as well as young men receiving visions" A genuine move of the Spirit is not ageist. All generations will experience the presence and power of God.

Thirdly, all social levels are included. There is not a special dispensation for the middle-classes or those socially acceptable or educated. The outpouring of the Spirit includes everybody, including "bond-servants". In the culture of the New Testament, this would mean that people who we might call "slaves" are included in this outpouring. It genuinely is for "all". *(Acts 2:39).*

The other observation I would make concerns the issue of race. Although this is not not mentioned by Peter in his preaching. The context tells us there were people from many different nations present, representing a number of cultures and different shades of skin colour. *(Acts 2:7-11).* The Spirit does not discriminate according to race. It may be for the "Jew first" but clearly "all flesh" *(Acts 2:17)* means exactly that.

3. Resulting Salvation.

The final and affirming evidence of a move of the Holy Spirit must result in men and women coming into a relationship with God through the Lord Jesus Christ. Unless salvation happens, I question the reality of what we call a move of the Holy Spirit. *(Acts 2:21)*. It is not the real thing! One of the privileges I have enjoyed over the past 20 years is to have travelled to many nations of the world, teaching and preaching. One of the joys is to see what God is doing in India, Nepal, the Philippines, Uganda and other African countries. The mark of the activity of the Holy Spirit is that many, in bible language "multitudes", are coming to the Lord. This must be the focus and expectation of an outpouring of the Holy Spirit. "Pentecost Now" means people constantly coming into a relationship with God. *(Acts 2:21)*.

The challenge presented by this is for us to encounter and experience another Pentecost; a new and vital relationship with the Holy Spirit. After all Peter did say. "It's for you" *(Acts 2:38,39)*.

O God of burning cleansing flame
Send the fire
Your blood-bought gift today we claim
Send the fire today
Look down and see this waiting host
And send the promised Holy Ghost
We need another Pentecost
Send the fire today – William Booth

2

LIGHTNING FROM HEAVEN

A few months later, in July of that same year, I was speaking at one of our churches when I was encouraged again to expect an outpouring of the Spirit. One Sunday morning, Caroline came forward to share a word of encouragement that she felt the Lord had given her. This was not a regular occurrence, in fact I had never heard her bring any public contribution before. She introduced herself as a scientist, which immediately caught my attention, and went on to describe an experience she had during the previous week. She described how she had been in her garden as several electric storms had broken out during that week, thunder and lightning, followed by storms impacting and affecting everybody within range. She then described her thoughts as she considered the source and rationale behind lightning. She described how thunder and lightning are a result of a build up of power in the heavens. Electric power builds up and then explodes, causing the sound of thunder and flashes of light. She then began to explain to us that there are two main forms of lightning, sheet or flash lightning and forked lightning sometimes called a lightning bolt. The sheet lightning occurs when the power builds up in the heavens but does not find an outlet so merely explodes in the sky. It makes one sit up and notice but does not make an impact on the earth; it is sometimes called cloud to cloud lightning. However, forked lightning happens when the power that is in the heavens finds an access point on earth which scientists call "a leader". The power that is in the heavens then makes an impact on the earth and often causes damage. She explained how often you will see a wispy thread of lightning emerge from the earth to connect with a powerful source of light striking from the heavens. This, we were informed, is the access point for the power that is in the heavens to affect the earth and it is called "a leader".

As I listened, I became immersed in my own thoughts as I felt inspired by the image that was being presented to me: that God had released His Power in the heavens and was looking for access points on the earth in order that His power might be manifested on the earth and do damage to the kingdom of darkness. God was looking for "leaders" through whom he could work in these days.

I began to pray about these "leaders" and ask God what

attracts His power that is in the heavens to make an impact on the earth. I also accessed pictures of lightning which invigorated my sense of excitement. I include a series of pictures that accentuate the prophetic picture of the power in the heavens accessing the earth. In the picture below a tree has become the "Leader" - the access point for the power that is in the heavens to impact the earth.

I began to meditate on the scriptures over this matter of thunder and lightning. My research uncovered that on a number of occasions in the Word of God, God manifests His powerful presence on the earth through Thunder and Lightning. There is a parallel between the natural picture and the supernatural invasion of the earth by God.

Moses was called up to meet with God on Mount Sinai. God's presence was manifested in thunder and lightning flashes; it says "the whole mountain quaked violently". *(Ex.19:9-20 (NASB)* It is not insignificant to note the constant use of phrases such as "God came down with the sound of thunder". His awesome presence was expressed in this phenomena.

When Israel asked for a king and God granted their request Samuel reprimands the people for their lack of trust in God and calls for thunder and rain. In response to the answer from heaven it says the people "greatly feared the Lord". It was seen as evidence of His presence invading the earth. *(1Sam.12:17,18)*

Elijah was engaged in spiritual warfare with the prophets of Baal and the challenge was for the true God to answer by fire from heaven. *(1Kings 18:20-39)*. As Elijah calls on God for Him to manifest His power and presence, a thunderbolt from heaven consumes the sacrifice, the altar and the water that has been poured over them. God's presence is again made clear by lightning.

Jesus, following the raising of Lazarus from the dead, was affirmed by the Father as a voice from heaven affirmed His pleasure with the Son. The surrounding crowd thought they heard thunder. Again there is this aligning of God making Himself known on the earth with thunder. *(1Kings 18:20-39)*. On a previous occasion as Jesus is baptised and the Holy Spirit comes upon Him there is a voice from heaven affirming the Father's pleasure in the Son. *(Luke 3:21)*

In the book of Revelation we have constant references to the Throne of God which is surrounded by flashes of lightning and peals of thunder. *(Rev.4:5,8:5,10:3,11:19)*.

Perhaps the most dramatic of these is expressed in chapter eight where in response to the activity of earth the angel releases thunder and lightning which impacts the earth in a powerful way. Again the parallel between God manifesting His presence and power on the earth with the thunder and lightning is clear.

I find it interesting that in our present society, dramatic scenes in film and TV are often accompanied by an electric storm and often it is related to the manifestation of evil and creates fear. The Bible has an alternative view of thunder and lightning; it is an indication of God making Himself known on earth!

With these thoughts I began to ask the question. If the power of God has been released in the heavens, what are the leaders that attract the power that is in the heavens and cause it to make an impact on the earth?

3

LIGHTNING AND LEADERS

The following is the beginning of an attempt to answer that question. I am sure there are many other "leaders" but here are my suggestions.

1. Faith.

It is clear to me that everything starts and finishes with faith. Faith in God, His Son and His Word. A total confidence in a God who still speaks and reveals His prophetic purpose to His people. I believe this is a foundation from which we begin as we look for those things that will attract the Holy Spirit.

In the book of Hebrews the writer lays a simple foundation for accessing the favour of God:

"That without faith in God it is impossible (the Greek word

used here literally means "we are impotent"), *to please God."* (Hebs. 11:6, James 1:8, Mark 11:24)

That same chapter speaks of the heroes who accessed the presence of God and saw extraordinary things happen on the earth through their lives and ministries. It says of every single one of them that it was "by faith". Enoch, Noah, Abraham, Moses, Gideon, David.... the list goes on. They were heroes who by faith saw God do extraordinary things on the earth as the power that is in the heavens found an access point. The Red Sea opened; Jericho collapsed; Elijah called fire and rain from heaven. Faith saw Naaman the leper healed and a young boy raised from the dead.

Faith becomes the foundation for us becoming "a leader" who attracts the power that is in the heavens. Regarding the Baptism of the Spirit and level of relationship we have with the Holy Spirit, Paul emphasises that we receive this through faith. *(Gal.3:14)*

I am confident that this God still speaks, and when we respond to His Word in faith we access the prophetic promise that He releases to us. I travel to Kampala, Uganda and often visit the Namirembe Christian Fellowship. The leader of the church is Simeon Kayiwa, who is a remarkable man. He has seen extraordinary miracles through his ministry over many years. At the entrance to the building is a prophetic word that he received at the beginning of his ministry approaching 40 years ago. It speaks of miracles, of many coming to salvation and healings taking place. I believe this has happened because he received by faith this word from God and he accessed the thunder and lightning of God upon his ministry. There is one miracle he speaks of when a thunderbolt was literally released from the heavens and struck a witchdoctor, killing him instantly.

As I understand this matter of faith, it will be as we take hold of this prophetic word from God and believe it, then we shall see its truth released on the earth.

Everything starts with faith.

2. Becoming a "Leader".

I was taken with this dramatic picture of lightning striking the statue of "Christ the Redeemer" that stands high on a mountain overlooking Rio je Janeiro, Brazil. It seemed to be a prophetic picture of the "leader" that God is looking for. It is not without significance that Jesus is the most powerful example of someone who accessed the power that was in the heavens and made the most significant impact on the earth of any man in history. It was after

Jesus was baptised by John in the river Jordan that the Holy Spirit descended upon Jesus in the form of a dove. *(Luke 3:21,22)*. It was then that the heavens opened and the Father spoke His approval and affirmation of His son, declaring that He was to be listened to. The next verse is also of importance, when it declares that Jesus BEGAN his ministry. *(Luke 3:23)*. It was not until the Holy Spirit had come upon Him that Jesus commenced His work of bringing healing and restoration to a broken world. *(Luke 4:18-21)*. He declares that it is because the Holy Spirit has empowered Him that He is now able to impact the world. That emphasises to me the importance of us being filled with the Holy Spirit.

If Jesus only began His ministry after His encounter with the Spirit, how much more do we need to access the power that is in the heavens to complete the work on earth?

This "leader" is not to do with position or titles. Being appointed to a role, given a job or completing a training programme does not make this kind of leader, although all these things have their place. The leader here is the one who makes themselves available to be a channel for the power that is in the heavens; the one who accesses the power that has been released in the heavens. It is about availability not position.

Isaiah is an excellent example when He comes into the presence of God. *(Is.6:1-10)*. He has an encounter with "thunder and lightning" as the presence of God fills the temple. He sees the throne of God, and the impact of the revelation causes him to cry out as he becomes aware of his uncleanness in the presence of a Holy God. The angel takes fire from the altar and touches his lips, cleansing him. He is anointed with fire. He then hears the voice of the Lord crying out for someone who would make themselves available. He responds by affirming his willingness to be a "leader" as he declares, *"Here am I, send me"*. He becomes a channel for the power of God to work through and we have the results of his extraordinary prophetic ministry for us inscribed in the chapters of this book. His revelation of the coming Christ, of His ministry, death, resurrection and the future kingdom are second to none. He is quoted by preachers and teachers of the Word of God, read publicly and referred to as much as any other of the sacred texts. God found an available instrument to impact with His Spirit who left an indelible impression on the earth.

The criteria for accessing the power that is in the heavens has more to do with availability than power, position, or any form of ego. In Ezekiel *(Eze 22:23-31. Nb:30)* it speaks of God looking among the different levels of leadership in the nation, among the prophets, the priests, the princes and even the ordinary people, but He did not find anyone available to be a connection point with the earth.

Isaiah understood what God was looking for in "leaders". He describes God as looking towards one who is humble, contrite of Spirit and who trembles at His word. *(Is.66:2)* This is the opposite of being arrogant, self-assured and self-confident. So many of the models that are presented to us as examples of leadership misunderstand the importance of humility - the need for a total dependence upon God and His power. It is not surprising that we are so lacking in power. Peter, as he writes his epistle near the end of his life and ministry, speaks clearly of the need for a right attitude if God is to trust us and grace us with His Spirit. *(1Pet.5:5,6.)*

D.L. Moody was an extraordinary man who God used powerfully to impact the 19th century church. Many thousands of people encountered the power of God as they heard him preach the Word of God. He was a simple man, poorly educated, who came into a relationship with God as a result of his Sunday School teacher sharing the gospel with him. He immediately set about establishing a work among the children of Chicago which developed into a church. He worked hard and was driven in his passion for God. However, it was after He accessed the power that is in the heavens that his ministry moved into another dimension. He made an impact upon his generation both in the USA and around the world.

The following passage from a book written by his spiritual son, R.A. Torrey describes how he was touched by the power of the Holy Spirit.

In his small book, <u>Why God Used D.L. Moody</u>, R.A. Torrey, writes about "the definite enduement from on high" that empowered Moody's preaching.

"The seventh thing that was the secret of why God used D. L. Moody was that: *he had a very definite enduement with power from on High, a very clear and definite baptism with the Holy Ghost.* Mr. Moody knew he had "the baptism with the Holy Ghost"; he had no doubt about it. In his early days he was a great hustler, he had a tremendous desire to do something, but he had no real power. He worked very largely in the energy of the flesh. But there were two humble Free Methodist women who used to come over to his meetings in the YMCA. One was "Auntie Cook" and the other, Mrs. Snow. These two women would come to Mr. Moody at the close of his meetings and say: "We are praying for you." Finally, Mr. Moody became somewhat nettled and said to them one night: "Why are you praying for me? Why don't you pray for the unsaved?" They replied: "We are praying that you may get the power." Mr. Moody did not know what that meant, but he got to thinking about it, and then went to these women and said: "I wish you would tell me what you mean," and they told him about the definite baptism with the Holy Ghost. Then he asked that he might pray with them and not they merely pray for him.

Auntie Cook once told me of the intense fervour with which Mr. Moody prayed on that occasion. She told me in words that I scarcely dare repeat, though I have never forgotten them. And he not only prayed with them, but he also prayed alone. Not long after, one day on his way to England, he was walking up Wall Street in New York (Mr. Moody very seldom told this and I almost hesitate to tell it), and in the midst of the bustle and hurry of that city his prayer was answered; the power of God fell upon him as he walked up the street and he had to hurry off to the house of a friend and ask that he might have a room by himself. In that room he stayed alone for hours; and the Holy Ghost came upon him, filling his soul with such joy that at last he had to ask God to withhold His hand, lest he die on the spot from very joy. He went out from that place with the power of the Holy Ghost upon him, and when he got to London, the power of God wrought through him mightily in North London, and hundreds were added to the churches, and that was what led to his being invited to the wonderful campaigns that followed in later years."

D. L. Moody himself testified to having a personal "baptism of the Holy Spirit" that changed his life and ministry. He is also credited with the following statement. *"The world has yet to see what God will do through a man totally consecrated to Him and by God's grace I aim to be that man."*

It seems that in these days, God is looking for men and women who will make themselves available to Him to be filled with the Holy Spirit in order to make an impact upon this generation.

3. Prayer and Praise.

The next "leader" I sensed was the dynamic of prayer and praise working together to produce a powerful conductor for the power of God to enter the human arena.

Paul and Silas had been preaching the good news about Jesus in Philippi and ended up in prison having been beaten with rods and put into prison with their feet in stocks. Most of us would have been complaining and groaning at such treatment but we find them praying and singing hymns of praise to God. The scripture says "suddenly" there came an earthquake. God broke in, His presence was revealed, everyone's chains fell off and all the doors were opened. *(Acts 16:22-26).* It was in response to prayer and praise that God manifested His powerful presence in the prison. Worship and intercession are an attraction that God responds to and so breaks in among His people.

In the book of Revelation we have a graphic insight into the activity of heaven, as earth becomes a "leader" to attract the power that is in the heavens through prayer and praise. *(Rev.8:2-5).* In this dramatic scene an angel holding a golden censer is given incense to add to *"the prayers of all the saints".* Incense throughout the scripture speaks of worship. These together come up before God, the angel is then released to fill the censer with fire from the altar and throw the censer to earth, which results in *"peals of thunder and sounds and flashes of lightning and an earthquake".* This prophetic picture encourages us to

29

understand what happens as we engage in these spiritual activities. Heaven responds to the leader of prayer and praise with activity on the earth.

Notice it is not prayer **or** praise but prayer **and** praise. It is not either/or but both/and. There needs to come a seamless transition between prayer and praise. We seem to separate these activities into praise times and prayer times. As I read the Psalms I find the writer moving from one to the other with a simplicity and confidence.

I believe by our separation of these "leaders" we have missed so much of what God wanted to do among us. I am sure you have heard of a lightning conductor. This is a metal rod connected to the top of a building and the wire, usually copper, connected to the ground away from the building. This attracts the lightning and takes the power away from the building and results in the energy harmlessly going into the ground. I think because we often separate praise from prayer we experience the same phenomena. *"Praise brings the presence of God; prayer releases the power of God."* Often our praise attracts the presence of God. We have great meetings, great times of encountering the presence of the Lord and go away satisfied with His presence. I believe God wants us to recognise the need to engage with presence and allow His power through prayer to fully explode on the earth. Turning presence into power through Holy Spirit led activity is a significant leader.

4. Corporate body empowered for service.

I love the picture below that speaks of a multiple invasion of the earth by the power that is in the heavens. I believe this illustrates what happened on the day of Pentecost when we are told a group of believers met together in unity and harmony and established a "leader" where God could come with the power of the Holy Spirit and invade the earth. The results of that invasion are still reverberating around the world as new outpourings of the Holy Spirit impact the church in the nations. *(Acts 2:1-4).*

David, in the Psalms has this wonderful revelation: that when the people of God come together in unity, the oil (a type of the Holy Spirit), flows and God comes and commands blessing. *(Ps.133:1-3).* A people joined together in unity and harmony is a foundational requirement for an invasion of the Spirit.

There are other qualities that attract the power that is in the heavens but these four were the ones that impressed themselves on me. I pray we will become the "leaders" both as individuals and churches that attract the power and presence of the Holy Spirit.

4

PURPOSE OF THE ANOINTING
EZEKIEL 47

Although it was that Pentecost Sunday in Uganda that prompted my concentrating on sharing the message of the Holy Spirit, it was not the beginning of my journey, as you will see. God had been speaking to me over the years about an outpouring of His Spirit and preparing us, His people, for this event.

It was in May 2013 that I prepared a message on the "Purpose of the anointing" after several months of being prompted by fresh insights shared with me from Ezekiel 47. *(Eze.47:1-12).*

The Bible is an amazing book. I have been studying it for over 50 years. I have certainly read this chapter over 50 times in my daily reading programme and heard numerous message preached, sung many songs based on this passage. Yet I heard something new and fresh that challenged me to pray and look with fresh understanding into this passage.

I was in a small gathering for leaders in the East Solent region when one of the young leaders shared what God had been saying to him from this portion of scripture. He said that as he read, he noticed the constant reference to the east, the constant references to the river flowing east and impacting the east. This grabbed his attention and he began to ask what does the east represent. Those of us who are involved in Bible study know that when in the Hebrew language something is repeated it usually stresses that this is important and must be taken notice of. In each of the first 3 verses of the chapter the flow of the water towards the east is mentioned and in verse 8 it is emphatically stated, as the river brings healing and life to the eastern region. The young man had then pursued what the east represented in the scriptures and was led to the book of Genesis where a revelation unfolded that brings understanding to us about the purpose of the Holy Spirit in our lives and new focus for the anointing of the Holy Spirit upon us.

1. The East is away from God.

He discovered that the east represents moving away from God, rebellion against God, disobedience to God, opposition to God and being out of the presence of God. We see all of this in the first few chapters of Genesis as well as in other places in the Word of God. Adam and Eve were driven out of the garden of Eden towards the east. *(Gen. 3:24)*. Their disobedience is associated with the east. Cain, following his actions which led to the murder of his brother, leaves the presence of God. *(Gen. 4:16)*. It is remarkable how it is stated *"he went out from the presence of the Lord and settled east of Eden"*. The relationship of being out of the presence of the Lord and in the east is unmistakable.   Nimrod builds Babylon. *(Gen. 10:8-10, 11:2.)*. Babel or Babylon throughout the scripture becomes synonymous with opposition to God and rebellion against God. It is also related to antichrist. Again it is stated clearly that the establishing of Babylon was part of a deliberate move east.

Abraham is called from the east. *(Gen. 12:1)*. He came from Ur of the Chaldees, part of Babylonia. Easton quotes in his Bible dictionary "Ur was consecrated to the worship of Sin, the Babylonian moon-god". He comes from a society drenched in idol worship opposed to God. God calls him out of the east. It is fascinating to see how this works through in his dealings with his nephew Lot. There was strife between their herdsmen so Abraham suggests they separate and offers Lot first option on the land. *(Gen.13:7-11. :12,13. 19:1.)* We read that Lot chose the valley of Jordan and journeyed eastwards! He ends up in Sodom which along with Gomorrah is destroyed by God because of its extraordinary wickedness. He moves away from God and its association with the east is clear.

The final example in Genesis relates to Ishmael. The illegitimate son of Abraham. It is prophesied of him that he will be wild and rebellious and makes the point that he will live to the east of all his brothers. *(Gen.16:12-15, 25:12-18 (NASB).* In his obituary again reference is made to the east alongside a reference that he settled in defiance of his relatives. He is also the father of the Arab nations and even today the effects on the world in which we live is still being felt.

What an amazing revelation! The east represents being out of the presence of God, away from God and in rebellion to God. As I have continued to meditate upon this there have been other confirmations. The Wise Men or more correctly, magi, arrive from the east. *(Matt.2:1.)*

There is much sentimental nonsense that surrounds these visitors from the east; they were involved in the occult; they were astrologers, they did not receive revelation from the Bible but rather in some extraordinary way the Holy Spirit broke into their understanding through their study of the stars that the appearance of this particular one was significant. The word "magi" is the same word from which we get our word magic! The east was associated with involvement in activities which were in direct opposition to God and motivated by demonic forces. They came out of the east, found the one who is the Way, the Truth and the Life and fell on their knees to worship Him. *(Matt. 2:11).* They came out of the darkness that the east represents, saw the light and bowed the knee in submission to the Son of God.

Another confirmation of this truth I discovered as I was reading the scriptures. The children of Israel are encouraged to walk in the light of the Lord and not be filled with the influences from the east which include occult activity. *(Is.2:5,6)*.

Maybe like me this was the first time you have heard this. I know I was surprised by this overwhelming evidence of what the east means. Having come to this understanding it is now important to relate it to our chapter in Ezekiel.

2. The Anointing is for the East.

Now as we look at the river that flows to the east we understand that the purpose of the anointing of the Spirit is for those who are away from God and His presence: those in disobedience, rebellion and even opposition to God and His ways. As we know from the scriptures, water, particularly flowing water, is a picture or type of the Holy Spirit. *(Is.44:3, John 7:37-39.)* When we see the association of the flowing river and the east we see clearly that God is anointing us by His Spirit for the sake of the lost and broken; those out of relationship with Him.

One of the things that concerns me as I look back over the last 20 years is that when God has come among us by the Holy Spirit the church has often responded by becoming self-centred and self- indulgent as they have just kept coming back for more personal blessing. I remember with affection the times of refreshing that were associated with Toronto. We laughed and cried, shouted and shook as we encountered the Holy Spirit. Many were healed up, set free and released from so much during those times - but what happened? Looking back, I believe we became self- obsessed with seeking more blessing; self-indulgently coming for more. We had not understood that the blessing was for the east. We stopped short of purpose. We lost the potential of the move of the Spirit because we did not understand God was empowering us for the sake of lost men and women. As I read Ezekiel 47 I was intrigued by the description of the flowing river that described the increasing depth of the river until it was deep enough to swim in. It struck me that we had enjoyed the "waters to swim in"; we had been blessed, been healed up, been set free, laughed and cried but stopped short of purpose. The river flowed on until it touched the stagnant, polluted waters of the east, where it impacted everything it touched.

What I saw and understood was that the purpose of anointing is for cleansing of the east. *(Eze.47:9-11). It says that "every place the river goes will live. The waters become fresh or healed".* People whose lives are dark, difficult and broken are cleansed, healed and set free. Very many fish are there. This relates to the emphasis in the ministry of Jesus where he often speaks to his disciples using the analogy of fishing as a picture of reaching needy people. This flow of life brings life where there has been death. The purpose of the anointing is for healing *(Eze. 47:12) p*eople being made whole. I believe this present emphasis on healing is no accident. It is a sign that we are hearing from God as many churches are engaging with people on the streets who are broken and hurting (from the east) and bringing healing and wholeness to them.

We exist for this. God has given us of His Spirit for the sake of people in need. The purpose of the anointing is for provision. It speaks of "food" being provided, God meeting people's needs. One of the other encouraging signs is the people of God being involved in caring and providing for people in a variety of caring ministries including the provision of food. God has poured out His Spirit upon us for the sake of the people who are away from Him.

I guess even if you struggle with some of the conclusions in this chapter, you will find it difficult to argue with Jesus Himself, who in a few words said exactly what I have been saying above. *(Luke 4:18,19)*. He made it clear that the anointing upon Him was for the sake of others: the sick, the oppressed, the bruised, the broken, the poor. The Holy Spirit comes upon us for the sake of those in the east.

To bring this chapter to a close, I would just like to make one or two observations.

First of all, it is noticeable that the further east the water went the deeper water became. I suggest the more we are involved with reaching lost and broken people, the more anointing we will know; the more healing we will see; the greater release of miracles and the supernatural we will experience.

The second thing is that we will not see the great ingathering of fish if the waters do not reach the east. In the ESV version verse 9 says, *"There will be very many fish…. once the waters reach there."* If we do not reach out and touch those outside of Christ we will not be a part of the outpouring that God wants us to know. How will they hear or know the presence of God if we do not go to where they are?

When I shared this message in Mumbai, India, the church was deeply challenged and engaged with a slum area literally east of their church building. The leaders, already challenged to reach out, engaged in 5 nights of outreach and evangelism. They saw 355 people make a response to Jesus and over 17 confirmed healings as up to 72 of them went east into their city.

We must recognise the call, realign ourselves with His purpose, receive the anointing of the Spirit and move into a season of reaping a harvest as we reach out to broken and hurting people.

5

"OLD MEN DREAM DREAMS"

One of the marks of the coming of the Spirit is that "old men will dream dreams". *(Acts 2:17)* It was a few years ago I became aware that I had moved from the vision stage that belongs to young men, to the place where I was considered "old", in that I had a series of dreams over a period of several months.

I had been planning to visit South Africa for a three week ministry trip. Plans were in hand, fares paid and a busy itinerary planned in various centres in that great country. Just a few weeks before I was to fly out I developed a serious eye problem. I was playing golf when my right eye was filled with blood from an internal bleed. I went immediately to the hospital to be told I had developed a torn retina that needed treatment urgently. I went through a horrible operation where the problem was dealt with but as a result of this surgery I was advised not to do anything but rest. During the operation a gas was put into the eye that had to dissolve before I could think of any serious work. When we visited the surgeon to ask about travelling to South Africa, he warned that if we flew, excruciating pain would develop within a few thousand feet and by the time we reached 10000 feet my eye would explode and its contents be spread around the cabin. We felt that the Lord was probably suggesting we did not travel at that time. This left me with an empty diary and time to rest, recuperate and meditate.

It almost seems as though this space enabled God to "get through to me" outside the busy agenda of the normal church leader's programme. I had a series of dreams, some of which I am committing to paper in this book. All of the dreams were related to the presence of God coming and the Holy Spirit invading and intruding our normal church meeting structure and programme.

The first and main dream was as follows:

In my first dream I was walking towards a meeting place with a group of others who I knew to be leaders. I was holding some keys and had an awareness that I was part of a team going to observe the meeting. I was expecting a Bible study type gathering with around 60 people present. It was a great surprise to walk into a large hall with several thousand people in banked seating like a football stadium. There was no music playing, no platform at the front of the building but an overwhelming sense of the presence of God filled the atmosphere, so much so that we all took a step back amazed at the intensity of the presence of God. It was as if the people were waiting for God to come. Then flashes of light began to move over sections of the congregation, spontaneously and unpredictably. As the light broke out over the people they burst into loud clapping as they were touched by the presence of God. There was an electric sense of anticipation such as I had never seen and the meeting had not even begun!

We then found ourselves walking into another gathering, this time at the back of the platform of a vast gathering that spread as far as the eye can see. Again the same sense of the powerful, presence of God was in the place. It seemed like the gathering started in a building but then opened up into the open air and an open field where tens of thousands of people were being touched by the presence of God. I became aware that this was bigger than one individual, church or network of churches. It was in this gathering on the right and left that I saw a couple of my relatives, which was a surprise to me.

The group I was with then moved into another gathering, this time in a church building. We entered the hall by a door located approximately half way down on the right hand side. A mature guy was teaching the Word of God. We murmured our approval at the excellent quality of teaching that was being presented. It was obvious this was a man of good grounding who understood the truth and had an ability to expound the scriptures. However, there was an increasing sense of frustration as he continued to speak. It was as if there was something he wanted to express that was locked up in him. Suddenly he said, "Where is the piano"? (I guess this dates me as in our modern context he would ask where was the keyboard!) He turned round and saw the piano; he went, sat down and began to sing. Out of his mouth came the most profound and powerful release of Bible truth. As he sang, it was as if a stream of water had broken through a dam. This prophetic truth unlocked something from heaven and at the same time the Holy Spirit came and the same sense of presence we had previously encountered broke out. There were some 300 people in the gathering and the Holy Spirit began to touch them, many crying and weeping, others lying prostrate on the floor, some laughing uncontrollably but all aware of the visible and powerful evidence of God breaking into peoples lives. This meeting then came to an end.

I then found myself behind the worship team in the same meeting room, preparing for the next gathering. They were tuning up and adjusting the PA when a lady from our church called Katrina, seated about half way towards the back of the hall, got up from her seat and began to walk towards the worship band. She held in her hand a small piece of paper about the size of a business card. When she arrived at the front of the hall she came over to the worship leader and passed the card to him with the words, "I was awake in the night and the Holy Spirit said we should sing these songs". There were about 4 songs written on this card. The worship leader took the card showed it to the band members and pointed to the first song saying, "Let's start with this one". They began to lead worship and before they arrived at the end of the first line the Holy Spirit broke in again and began to touch the lives of all those present in the meeting, many having major encounters with the presence and power of God.

Our next meeting place was a smaller hall holding around 70 people. I knew they were all church leaders. They were praying and calling on God to come. They were reaching out to the Lord for a move of the Holy Spirit. Many of those present were using the Psalms where hunger for God and His presence are expressed. I saw that over in the corner there were some people being prayed for. I moved towards them and was surprised to see a couple I know very well being ministered to. People were prophesying over them and praying for them. They had been leaders in the church in Belgium but had returned to their own country. During their time in Belgium God has used them significantly during the mid-90's and the times of refreshing. I felt a prophetic stirring and went over to pray with them. They were both lying on their backs side by side. As I knelt beside them I began to prophesy, "You are a carrier of revival, a carrier of a move of the Holy Spirit. You have laid down the spirit of revival that you once had. You have been wounded, become disillusioned and hurt but deep within you there is a desire and hunger for God that has not been lost. The flame has not gone out, although it is now just a flickering light. There is a longing in you for God to come again in power". I then began to quote those same Psalms, "When shall I appear before God"?; "My heart and my flesh cry to the living God"; "as the deer pants for the water so my soul longs after you". I became aware of a deep cry coming from within this couple and aware also of tears running down my face. In fact, the whole room of leaders were weeping as they were reaching out to God. They were not tears of regret or remorse but tears of joy and expectation as there was an awareness that God had heard the cry of their hearts and was coming to touch them again.

Suddenly I found myself in a car park where several coaches were parked. I saw a young woman of mixed race standing by one of the coach doors. She was looking at me, and I heard a voice saying, "This is your granddaughter". I was some 10 yards away and surprised by this statement as the young lady was obviously not from my immediate family, her features indicating she was not initially from England. She saw my surprise and said, "You do not see how I can be your granddaughter do you?" I replied, "No". She then said, "Let me tell you my story. I never knew who my father was and my mother abandoned me when I was 3 years old. I went from foster home to foster home. In my early childhood I was physically abused; I never knew what it was to be loved. As I approached my teenage years I was sexually abused and misused. By my mid-teens I was on the streets, selling my body as a prostitute to earn the money to buy drugs and alcohol that dulled the pain and inner agony I experienced. I had never known true love. Then several years ago someone introduced me to Jesus. I at last knew what it was to be loved; He cleaned me up, set me free, released me from all the damage of the past and put me in a family, His family. That's why I am your granddaughter. It was your sons and daughters that introduced me to Jesus." I was weeping as she told me this story. I then woke up!

I lay in bed overwhelmed by the dream, aware that it was significant, but totally overcome with emotion by this powerful encounter. Over the following weeks I prayed and meditated over its significance, after all it was only a dream and yet I knew it was more than that! These are a few conclusions I have come to:

1. I was in it and part of it. There would be a move of the Holy Spirit that I would participate in!

2. The first room with no platform, preacher or worship band indicated that we can have all of the organisation and programmes, but unless we have the presence and power of the Holy Spirit everything else is just a substitute for the real thing.

3. The larger room breaking into a massive outdoor crowd indicates that this will not be just a local event but a move of the Holy Spirit across the churches.

4. The relatives I saw are significant. One is a backslider. They once walked with God but got disillusioned and

hurt by church, particularly through being mishandled by leaders. I felt the Lord say to me that they are coming back; that many prodigals, wounded and hurt by church, will return in this move of the Holy Spirit.

The other relative is a good, faithful church member. They have faithfully followed the Lord, done all the right things, believed all the right things, but never had a life-changing encounter with the person of the Holy Spirit. I felt that they represented an army of people in our churches for whom this is true. They will come alive as the Holy Spirit invades their lives.

5. In the next room, which seemed more like a local church, I believe the good, solid, faithful Bible teacher represents a multitude of faithful ministers who have remained true and fulfilled their ministry but seen little fruit. I believe that in the day of the Holy Spirit all the reservoir of truth and understanding locked up within them will come flooding out in a river of Holy Spirit life as they are touched by the Spirit as never before.

6. Katrina, the lady who left her seat, is one of the faithful servers in our church. She did head up the catering and hospitality in our local fellowship. I felt the Lord say that there were a host of people hiding behind a serving ministry, avoiding the challenge of both ministering directly into people's lives and expecting the Holy Spirit to use them. I felt that God is going to use an army of ordinary people in the supernatural. Healing, the prophetic, outreach will not just be the domain of the

professionals but God will take hold of people open and available to Him. I shared the dream with Katrina and her husband and since that time she has developed and blossomed in a number of areas of ministry including leading prayer ministry in our church, travelling to the developing world, teaching the Word of God, passionate about the work of God.

7. The leader and wife represent a number of leaders, burnt out and wounded by their experiences. I felt God was going to restore and revitalise numbers of disillusioned leaders, setting them on fire again, stirring up the embers of the fire that once burned.

> *"Lord please light the fire*
> *That once burned bright and clean*
> *Replace the lamp of my first love*
> *That burns with Holy fear"*
> *(O Lord you're beautiful, Keith Green. 1980)*

Finally, the scene in the car park. Why the sudden change from meetings to a public arena? Why this dramatic encounter with this young woman whose story of transformation was so powerful? I believe there is a simple application related to this move of the Spirit. All the presence and power, all the feelings and show of emotion, all the prophetic words and outpourings are for one purpose; to reach this lost, broken and hurting generation. This young woman of mixed race represents a multitude of people who desperately need Jesus to change and impact their lives. This move of the Spirit is for those who are hurting and wounded. Only those individuals and churches who understand that, will be part of this wonderful and powerful intervention of the Holy Spirit.

God is looking for a people to pour out His Spirit upon; a people who will impact this broken and hurting world.

6

MORE DREAMS

Over those three weeks I had a number of dreams that were all related to the presence of God invading the church to release the presence and power of the Holy Spirit. Some of them were about individuals and it is not appropriate to share them. The following I believe are interesting and appropriate to share.

In one of the dreams, I was in a large meeting place with a crowd of several thousand people. The building had a considerable platform and I was seated to the left of this stage and at the front. The meeting came to an end but I sensed in my spirit that God was not finished with the gathering and wanted to move in a greater and deeper way. The benediction was completed and as I sat in my seat I felt moved to stand, lift my hands and sway from left to right giving a wave offering before the Lord. As I continued, feeling rather foolish, I became aware of an increasing sense of the presence of God. I looked around and was surprised and encouraged to see a number of people around the auditorium engaged in exactly the same activity. I then felt that the Lord would have me to go onto the platform, request that I be allowed to use the microphone and encourage people to come up to encounter the Lord. I shared how that there were times when God came to particular places and made Himself known and that if people were to come to this place they would know His power and presence in their lives. As people began to come onto the platform they encountered the presence of God. Again people had powerful experiences with the Holy Spirit. All the manifestations I had seen in my previous dreams were again evident as God by His Spirit touched the lives of His people. This continued for a time and then the meeting began to come to a conclusion.

As I looked from the platform over to the right of the building I saw a lady I knew well enter the premises. This lady had a ministry in the area of music and worship and had established a successful choir. I knew she had been through some difficulties with this ministry and I heard later that she had also faced some serious health challenges. I felt moved to go over to where she was, lay hands on her and prophesy. I spoke of her disappointment and time of difficulty and then encouraged her to believe God for a new door of opportunity to open and that the dreams and visions she carried would be fulfilled. The Holy Spirit came upon her and she spent some time lying before the Lord on the carpet. The dream ended. I meditated upon the fact that God came outside of our planned meeting time, and felt encouraged to expect God to come by His Holy Spirit.

The following Sunday I was in a missions meeting following the usual church service. I had not seen the lady that appeared in the dream for several years. Imagine my surprise when she walked into this gathering. I felt constrained to share the dream with her and it was not surprising that tears began to run down her face as she requested that I prayed for her. I willingly did this and wait with anticipation to hear of the dealings of God with her since that time.

Another dream concerned a church I have been involved with on the south coast. I was with the church in their usual Sunday morning gathering when someone (I only heard the voice) suggested that the Lord wanted us to take His presence out onto the street. We concurred, and in the next scene we were gathered in a circle worshipping on the pavement in the same way as in the church building. There was a very real sense of the presence of the Lord as we sang and praised together. I then noticed 5 or 6 young people breaking into the circle and moving towards the young people of the church. It was obvious that they recognised them as they called them by name and asked what was going on and indicated that something was making an impression on them.

One of them was a young man, interestingly dressed and displaying some metal piercings and tattoos on his body. I felt constrained to address him, feeling inspired with a sense of prophetic inspiration. I moved towards him and said, "God loves you and is interested in your life, He knows all about you and your struggles and circumstances". At this the young man's eyes filled with tears and he asked me how I knew that. I continued to encourage him with prophetic encouragements that God was interested in breaking into his life and revealing Himself to this young man. I invited him to commit His life to the Lord Jesus to which he assented enthusiastically. I invited one of the young people of the church who knew the young man to lead him in a prayer of repentance.

I turned away and had a conversation with the Lord. It went something like this. "Lord what is going on? I have done this stuff for years, knocking on doors, stopping people on the streets and have seen so little in terms of response, yet this young man opened up so easily and willingly". I felt the Lord say, "It is a new season and the difference is My presence". I realised again that the purpose of the anointing is for the lost and broken.

That was some 3 years ago. During these past 2 weeks at the time of writing we have been on the streets of our home city, Southampton. Over 500 people have prayed inviting Jesus into their lives. This outreach was inspired by the story of what God has recently been doing in

Reading, Berkshire, where over 2000 people have responded to the Lord as the people from many different churches have shared their faith on the streets of the town.

Did I see this in my dream some years ago? Is this the fulfilment of what I saw? Again, the emphasis of this outreach is on the presence of God making the difference. It is not an evangelism based upon duty but upon the people of God coming into contact with His presence. There is a day of harvest clearly prophesied as a result of an outpouring of the Holy Spirit. We look for it, in our day and in this generation! *(Joel 2:21-32)*

In another dream I was called to a meeting in Central Hall, Southampton. A number of leaders were called together. The senior leadership requested that we pray over several matters. There were some difficult situations; some to do with breakdowns in relationships, several very sick people with life-threatening illness and some financial challenges. There was a feeling that we needed a Word from God. We were called to return the following week and share what we felt the Lord was saying. I treated this seriously and began to pray.

Every time I began to pray I felt the Lord say I should speak out confidently in tongues, the language of the Spirit. I argued with God asking what was the point and purpose in that! All that would happen would be I would be embarrassed and seen as being irrelevant. The day of the meeting arrived and several people shared their conclusions. All the contributions were good but I felt increasingly uncomfortable because I was being prompted and reminded of what God had said to me- that I was to speak out in tongues. In the end I could bear the pressure no longer and stood and said that all I had was this prompting to speak in tongues. As I did so, within seconds the presence of God broke out on the leaders in the room and around 30 of us encountered the presence of the Holy Spirit in various wonderful and inspiring ways. I found myself talking again to God, complaining that although this was great, what difference did it make. We still had all the issues facing us. His reply was simply that His presence made all the difference we needed. Relationships would be restored as people's hearts were touched; bodies would be healed as the Holy Spirit came; people's pockets would be touched to give and the financial need would be met; that an outpouring of the Holy Spirit would bring resolution to all those things that confronted us.

The history of revivals and moves of the Holy Spirit confirm what I saw in my dream: that many of our outstanding problems and difficulties are resolved when God comes. As people's hearts are changed by the power of the Holy Spirit working in them, so a new sensitivity to God begins to work in them. I have heard a number of prophecies that include the thought that when God breaks in, things that took 6 years would take 6 months; things that took 6 months would take 6 weeks; things that took 6 weeks would take 6 days. There was a promise of acceleration! This concurs with the promise in Amos where the whole process of harvest is speeded up as the one who sows the seed is overtaken by the one who reaps the harvest in the day when God raises up and restores His people. *(Amos 9:11-13, Acts 16:15-18).*

The final dream which I feel at lliberty to include in this chapter takes place in a church in Essex where I ministered over a number of years. There had been some difficulties in relationships and they had been so severe that some had felt that the only option was to leave and join another fellowship. These broken relationships had persisted for years. I was in a meeting in this one particular church when the Holy Spirit broke in and we experienced a dramatic move of God. The result of this was that there were some who felt moved to repent for their part in the break down in relationships that had occurred. They then felt that it was important to make contact with those who had left and were now part of another fellowship. As they made contact by telephone, they were amazed to find that exactly the same thing had happened in that church and the same desire to repair relationships had resulted. It was then that reports came from other churches in the region that a similar release of the Spirit had been manifested. There came an awareness that God had come; new life was springing forth from a people in right relationships who had dealt with resentment and bitterness; that out of the foundation of unity and harmony God was releasing a new wave of His Spirit. *(Ps. 133.)*

To bring this chapter to a conclusion you may be asking and wondering about the significance or reliability of dreams. They are all very subjective. Are these prophetic words from God? Is God speaking? Well I believe He is, but at the end of the day they are just dreams. I dream regularly about all sorts of things. I have crazy dreams, daft dreams, scary dreams and all kinds of other dreams. However, I am aware that from time to time I awake from a dream and sense that God is speaking through a dream.

The Bible in both Testaments is full of dreams where God communicates His mind, heart and will. In the case of these dreams that I received, all within a few weeks of one another, I do believe that God is speaking to us of His heart towards us for another Pentecost.

I will leave you to draw your own conclusions.

7

FRESH OIL

We held a prophetic conference at our church. One of our ladies was given the opportunity to share a prophetic word she believed the Lord had given her. She described how that as she was in prayer, the words "second pressing of the olive" had dropped into her mind. She had no idea what those words meant and no concept of their significance at that stage. As she waited on the Lord and researched the phrase, she understood that olive oil is produced by being pressed. The Bible itself has several mentions of the olive being pressed to produce oil. She then discovered that after oil has been produced the olives are left for a season before another pressing produces yet more oil. "The second pressing of the oil" is a common practice. As she further meditated on the issue, she felt the Lord was bringing a word of encouragement to those who are over 55 years of age. That God was coming to those of mature years with a fresh touch of His Holy Spirit. That the oil was going to flow and this older generation were going to be used afresh by God. She drew a parallel from the miracle at Cana when the headwaiter declared that "the best wine had been kept until the last" *(John 2:1-12)*. The years of faithful service, reading and receiving the Word of God, prayer and intercession were going to be rewarded with a fresh touch of the Holy Spirit and a season of fruitfulness such as this generation had not known.

As I listened to this word, I felt an immediate response in my spirit. There was a "yes" that echoed in my heart as it was so in line with all that God had been saying to me. It certainly was in accord with my dreams. I felt that it was probably a word for mature believers and might not need an age restriction but nevertheless was inspired to consider and meditate on the Word. The result was a message based on *Ps. 92: 10 (NASB)* where the psalmist speaks about being anointed with fresh oil.

The translation of this verse in various versions is interesting. The NIV says "fine oil"; BBE – "best oil"; NLT – "finest oil"; AV – "fresh oil"; NASB – "fresh oil". All of them indicating quality. This oil is not rubbish, it is the best. It is not the cheap, basic brand of the local supermarket but the finest, virgin oil of superior quality. It is not old and stagnant but fresh and alive. The Psalmist concurs with this in other places. The Shepherd

Psalm talks about being anointed with oil, as does another Psalm speaking of *"oil that makes the face shine or glisten" (Ps.23:5, Ps. 104:15.)*

There is nothing worse than old, worn out, used up, burnt out oil. On a recent trip to South Africa we followed a truck up a steep hill; it was billowing out black smoke and struggling to make it. My travelling companion commented, "That vehicle requires an oil change". The oil required replacing; the engine was not running smoothly or efficiently because it had not been serviced. When a car is serviced, one of the first requirements is an oil change to ensure its on-going effectiveness. The application for us all is that we need an oil change, an infusion of fresh oil to operate effectively as disciples of the Lord, constantly being "filled with the Holy Spirit". There is nothing dull and ineffective about fresh oil.

Another analogy about oil relates to the home. There is nothing worse than entering a house that reeks of stagnant, burnt, worn out oil; a kitchen where oil has been used over and over until the whole place is permeated with an unhealthy smell. A number of years ago there was the development of home fryers where food such as chips, French fries to our friends from the US, could be cooked in your own home in one of these pans. We purchased one but it was not long before my wife could no longer stand the smell that pervaded the home every time it was used and that then lingered around for hours.

It was soon passed on to another home, where I suspect the same thing happened. In fact, this wonderful invention seems to have disappeared! We need to get rid of the stale oil and replace it with fresh oil; the best oil. To visit a café, affectionately called a "greasy spoon" in the UK and be served an egg cooked in oil that has been used over and over and receive your food covered in black, burnt bits and pieces, is not a blessing.

For us as men and women of the Spirit, we need to constantly undergo an oil change to replace the stale oil with a fresh, new encounter with the living Jesus and His Holy Spirit, who wants to renew and revive us.

The scriptures give us two further pictures of this principle as they teach us about the importance of "new wine" and "flowing water". In several gospels Jesus spoke of the "new wine" that was coming as he contrasted the new and old, declaring the importance of new wineskins to retain the new wine. There is nothing worse than wine that has been left too long, wine that has "gone off". Its taste is bitter and sour. *(Luke 5:37,38)*. As mentioned in a previous chapter looking at Ezekiel 47, the fresh, living, flowing water attacks the stagnant, dead, putrid water and brings life and vitality. *(Eze.47:1-12)*.

One of the privileges of the ministry I have been engaged in is that I get to travel to the nations where we often meet with significant and extraordinary people serving God in leadership roles. In the USA I met with an amazing man. His name is Joel Laurore. We had originally met him some 10 years before on the island of Jamaica where we were involved together in a conference. We were so impressed by the anointing on this man that one night my wife and I sat up talking. We ended up talking together for the whole night, the first and only time in my life I have done that. We listened, prayed, wept and laughed together but the overriding memory is the story of his encounter with the Holy Spirit. Joel was a good Baptist. He was originally from Haiti but trained in the USA and completed a Phd degree and became a Doctor of Divinity. He was able to read the Greek language fluently and had an excellent grasp of Theology. As he spoke French, he was asked to become the Principle of the Western African Theological Seminary located in Liberia. For a number of years he fulfilled this task. Every Monday evening it was part of his responsibility to address the 100 students from 30 African countries who were studying at the college. He had personally reached the end of his resources; he felt weak and burnt out. Before he went out to address the students he poured out his heart to God in his study. His prayer was that if God did not turn up by His Spirit, then Joel was going to return home and become a teacher. He was dry and washed up, with nothing left to give. He entered the hall and stood to address the students. As he did so, the Holy Spirit fell upon him and he began to speak with other tongues in an energetic way. He found himself walking forwards and backwards across the platform speaking in various languages for over 2 hours. When he had come to an end of speaking he was amazed to discover that he had prophesied over every one of the 100 students in their own indigenous language as the Holy Spirit had anointed him with fresh oil. That was the beginning of an outpouring of the Spirit in Liberia in which many churches were planted, people found Jesus as Lord and thousands of Christians were filled with the Holy Spirit.

Now, years later, we were with this man in a church in Oklahoma and he is still alive in the Spirit, enjoying the freshness of the anointing of the Holy Spirit. Still alive and excited about the Lord even though he is approaching 80 years of age.

I believe God wants to anoint us afresh with his Holy Spirit and for the older generation to enjoy a new touch of God upon their lives. The hymn writer puts his aspiration like this:

"Where is the blessedness I knew when first I knew the Lord? Where is that soul-refreshing view of Jesus and His word?

"Return O Holy Dove! Return, sweet messenger of rest!" (*O for a closer walk with God – W. Cowper.*)

His cry is for the Holy Spirit to touch him again.

The value and benefit of this "fresh oil" are seen in the promises that the psalmist expects as a result of this new encounter with the Holy Spirit. *(Ps.92:11-14).*

1. Triumph over his enemies. A new surge of the power

of God that results in a turning around of his fortune.

2. Flourishing like a palm tree. The marginal reference in the NASB version gives an alternative of "sprout"; an expectation of coming to life; new life springing up where there has been barrenness.

3. Fruitfulness even in old age. I love the promise of still fruit bearing in later years. The NASB speaks of *"being full of sap and very green"*; healthy, productive, reaping a harvest as a result of continuing to be touched by the oil of the Holy Spirit.

It is interesting and worth commenting on, that as I studied this passage, my eyes were drawn to the title at the beginning of the Psalm where we are told this is a "Song for the Sabbath." *(Ps. 92:1-9.)* In other words this is a song they sang when they met together for praise and worship. The first verses speak of giving thanks to the Lord for His greatness and His works, of corporate singing and praising God. As you read into verse 10 the theme changes radically to the blessing of God upon the believer. As a result of praising God, His presence is released among His people and they are touched and blessed with "fresh oil". This concurs with Charismatic and Pentecostal theology that emphasises the importance of praise and worship as a mean of accessing the presence and power of God. *(Ps.22:3)*. The song, "Jesus we enthrone you" expresses exactly the same sentiments as the Psalmist.

"Jesus we enthrone you we proclaim you as King,
Standing here in the midst of us we lift you up with our praise
and as we worship build your throne,
come Lord Jesus and take your place".

This is why coming together and worshipping together is not an optional extra but an essential element of our walk with God that ensures we enjoy the fresh touch of Jesus upon our lives.

In the New Testament the writer of Ephesians encourages us to constantly be filled with the Spirit. *(Eph.5:18-19.)* He suggests as we sing songs of worship and use the language of the Holy Spirit and sing in other tongues we will be freshly filled with the Spirit. It is interesting that the encouragement is ambiguous and can be translated as "speaking to yourself" or "speaking to one another". In other words, both in the rhythm of our own private devotions and corporately in gatherings, we should receive "fresh oil".

In Pentecostal circles there was a tendency for a testimony to be shared as a list of spiritual achievements. Saved on a certain date, baptised in water on a following day and filled with the Spirit at some further event, almost like a passing of exams. However, the question is not, "were you filled with the Holy Spirit", but **are** you filled with the Holy Spirit today! Of both Peter and Paul who were initially filled with the Holy Spirit, the writer of Acts speaks of them being filled again or afresh with the

Spirit at given moments for different challenges. *(Acts 2:1-4, 4:8, 31. 9:17, 13:9).* I believe it was C.H. Spurgeon who when challenged why he kept referring to being filled again with the Holy Spirit answered simply, "Because I leak". That says it all. God wants to come to us again with a fresh touch of the Spirit.

The hymn writer Mrs C. H. Morris expressed it like this:

"Are you looking for the fullness of the blessing of the Lord in your heart and life today?

Claim the promise of your Father, come according to His word, In the Blessed old time way.

Bring your empty earthen vessels, clean through Jesus precious blood. Come you needy one and all, and in human consecration wait before the throne of God, till the Holy Ghost shall fall.

Like the cruse of oil unfailing is His grace for evermore and His love unchanging still. And according to His promise, with the Holy Ghost and power, He will every vessel fill.

He will fill your heart today to overflowing, As the Lord commanded, you bring your vessels not a few. He will fill your heart today to overflowing with the Holy Ghost and power."

8

THE SPIRIT AND POWER OF ELIJAH

In all the previous chapters I have spoken of recent events, dreams and prophetic messages that I believe the Lord has been giving me for the church.

However, in this chapter I am including a dream that goes back over 20 years. The year before the "Times of Refreshing" associated with Toronto broke out I had a very strong and significant dream. I was on my own faced by a coat on a coat stand. As I looked at the coat I observed that it was of a considerable size and certainly too big for me. I then heard a voice which I knew was the voice of God telling me to "put the mantle on". It was a strange request for 2 reasons, firstly because of the use of the word mantle rather than coat because it was just an ordinary coat. Secondly, it was far too big for me to wear. My response expressed my surprise and reluctance as I replied, "It is too big for me". Without any explanation the voice came again a little stronger. "Put the mantle on". Again I responded negatively. This went on for a little while with the voice becoming more and more insistent. Eventually I relented and, murmuring under my breath that it was too big for me, I went towards the coat and put it on. Imagine my surprise as I looked down to see that it fitted me perfectly. Then I woke up. I was quite taken with this dream and for several months waited on it, prayed over it and shared it with a number of my colleagues, none of whom had the slightest idea what it meant, if anything. I could not lay it down and would meditate on it regularly. After about 6 months we held a leaders' gathering and invited a brother from Chile, called Miguel Escobar, to address us. He opened his Bible at 1 Kings 19 and proceeded to read about Elijah. As he read the passage the word mantle appeared several times in the passage. *(1 Kings 19:9-19)*. It was as if a light went on and I could not believe that I had not connected the dream with the mantle of Elijah. This famous and well-known story of Elijah and his coat or mantle signifying the presence and power of the Holy Spirit. He connected Elijah's mantle with the story of Saul when the Holy Spirit came mightily upon him and he was changed in to another man. *(1 Sam. 10:6,7)*. I felt the Holy Spirit bringing this alive to me personally, that I was to experience a special anointing of the Holy Spirit. I heard very little else of the preacher as I considered the significance of the prophetic dream that I believed was from the Lord.

As I considered the dream, I began to realise it had a much broader application than just me personally. As the scriptures opened to me afresh, I remembered from restoration teaching in the late 70's and early 80's how we saw "the Spirit of Elijah" as a prophetic picture of the Holy Spirit coming upon the people of God before Jesus would return. It went something like this:

There is a prophetic thread through the scriptures of a people who will be anointed with the same "spirit and power as Elijah". It commences with Elisha. Elijah announces to Elisha that he will be taken to heaven today. *(2Kings.2:1-15)*. The two of them travel together, as they approach the river Jordan Elijah takes the mantle (coat) and strikes the water. The water opens and they cross over on dry ground. This confirms for us that the mantle is a symbol and type of the power and anointing of the Holy Spirit. After they have crossed the water Elijah asks Elisha what his aspiration is and he replies that he would appreciate a double portion of the Spirit that rests upon Elijah. Elijah assures him that if he sees him go to heaven he will receive that anointing. A chariot of fire appears and a whirlwind whisks Elijah off to heaven. We read that Elisha "saw it", so knew that his prayer had been granted. He picks up the mantle of Elijah that had dropped to the ground and begins to return. When he reaches the banks of the Jordan he takes the coat and strikes the water crying, "Where is the Lord, the God of Elijah?" The waters divide and Elisha knows that the Spirit has clothed him. As he returns, he is met by the sons of the prophets who say, "The spirit of Elijah rests on Elisha". The same spirit now rested on Elisha.

Moving to the beginning of the New Testament we find Zacharias, the priest, having an encounter with an angel. He is advised that he is to have a son who God is going to use to prepare for the coming of the Messiah, the Christ, the Anointed one. It is said of him that he will be "filled with the Holy Spirit while yet in his mother's womb and that he will be anointed with: "the spirit and power of Elijah". *(Luke 1:17).*

Jesus makes a mysterious and revealing reference to this in the gospel of Matthew. *(Matt. 17:10-13, 11:11-15.)* Jesus declares that Elijah is coming, in the future, but then says Elijah already came. The statements seem contradictory until you realise that Jesus is speaking of the "spirit and power of Elijah"; the empowering of the Holy Spirit. I do not believe that these scriptures speak of a literal returning of a physical Elijah, but rather the same anointing for ministry. That power had already come in the ministry of John the Baptist and will come upon a people in the future. That is clear from the passage here and earlier in the gospel. So we have this same empowering presence of the Spirit upon different generations… The same spirit that was on Elijah, rested upon Elisha and John the Baptist. It is also prophesied that this anointing will come again. *(Mal. 4:5).* Notice it is clear this will happen before the day of the Lord, before Jesus returns, before the end of time. There will be a movement of people filled with the spirit and power of Elijah. I believe it began on the day of Pentecost and has continued over and over again as the Spirit has come afresh upon each new generation.

Now today, I believe my dream was a prophetic encouragement to expect again a special outpouring of the Holy Spirit. When in the mid- 90's the Spirit was poured out in extravagant ways bringing us into a new awareness and expectation of His presence and power, I was encouraged that my dream was beginning to be fulfilled. That move of the Holy Spirit seemed to pass. I believe He comes again to encourage this generation to be filled with the Spirit and Power of Elijah.

What can we expect? Well it is worth a look into the life of Elijah. What will be the marks of a people touched by the "Spirit and power of Elijah?"

Ordinary People.

Elijah the Tishbite was an ordinary man. It is interesting that it does not say the spirit and power of any of the other great heroes of the Old Testament. Why not David, Moses, Joshua, Abraham, Nehemiah? Possibly because they were gifted, educated, powerful people. Elijah is an ordinary guy. He is a nobody from nowhere. We can all identify with that. The first time we read about Elijah we discover he is a Tishbite. *(1Kings 17:1)*. Although this sounds like a disease it is simply letting us know he was from Tishbe. This was a village in the area of Israel known as Gilead, which was a barren place on the wrong side of the Jordan. A farming community, unsophisticated, poorly educated and socially a less significant part of the country.

In Jewish tradition, if you were from the more significant parts of society and your family was well known and respected, you were known by the name of your father. So we have Joshua the Son of Nun, Benaiah the son of Jehoida, even Elisha the son of Shaphat, but Elijah is known by the town he came from. That does not mean he did not have a father but that his father had no significance in the society of the day. This anointing is for us ordinary people and as God anointed Elijah to impact a nation, and a nobody became a nation changer, I believe God will do the same with us. *(1Kings 18:39. 1 Cor.1:26-28)*.

History is littered with the stories of ordinary people from ordinary backgrounds who, anointed by the power of the Holy Spirit, achieved extraordinary things.

Spirit of God in human frailty.

The second reason I see Elijah as a model, is the Spirit of God coming upon us in spite of our human weakness and failings. Elijah is an ordinary man but also faces the same challenges as us. In the New Testament James speak of him as a man like us. *(James 5:17)*. He was an ordinary guy who struggled with the same things we do. In one chapter he is afraid, depressed, wanting to die and full of self-pity; he is not a super-hero. *(1Kings 19:3,4, 14)*. We find it easy to identify with this man because these are the same issues we are dealing with. They do not disqualify us from being used by the Lord.

People of prayer.

The importance of prayer in drawing on the resources of heaven is emphasised in the life of Elijah. The powerful ability to call on God in faith and see the release of the miraculous power of God is seen again and again in his life and ministry. He prayed that it would not rain and it did not rain for 3 years; he prayed again and it started. *(James 5:17,18. 1Kings 18:42-45)*. He called down fire from heaven. *(1Kings 18:36-38)*. What a challenge to understand the power of prayer in releasing God's power and authority on the earth.

People of prophetic influence and creative faith.

As you read of Elijah you have this sense of the effect he had on the world he which he lived. I believe God wants us to become communicators of His heart and mind; speaking into every area of life; walking in relationship with God; understanding the mind of God; speaking the word of God; believing God for the fulfilment of the prophetic word.

People preparing the way for the Lord.

Just as John the Baptist prepared the way for the first coming of the Lord so we, anointed with the same spirit, are called to prepare the way for the second coming of the Lord. (*Luke 1:17, 3:4-9*). Malachi prophecies of a people filled with the Spirit who will bring in the end of the age. (*Mal. 4:5*). This was partially fulfilled through John the Baptist but as we have previously seen Jesus told us He is coming. There will be another revelation of this ministry. My friend, John Noble in his excellent book on the Holy Spirit, gives a very powerful exegesis of Rev.12 in which he suggests that the 2 witnesses are not individuals but a body of people: the church filled with the word (Moses) and the Spirit (Elijah), releasing the power of God on the earth in the last days.[1]

People who impact the nation.

This people will turn the nations to God by the power of the Holy Spirit just as Elijah did. (*1Kings 18:39*). It is not insignificant that the major symbols of fire and water are involved in the major miracles of Elijah. They are both symbols of the Holy Spirit throughout the scriptures. I believe God wants to raise up a generation of fire and water carriers.

My friend, Paul Randerson, made a statement recently that our churches should be "presence centres which produce presence carriers," - God clothing us with the Spirit; the Spirit and Power of Elijah coming upon us to enable us to impact the nations.

---

[1] Everymans guide to the Holy Spirit the end of the world and you. – John Noble. 1991.(Kingsway Press)

9

CONCLUDING THOUGHTS

So there it is. It is not for me to say, "This is the Word of the Lord". It is for you, the reader to decide whether or not you can hear God in these dreams, thoughts and prophetic messages. Even if you do not agree with one point here or another over here, there is a bigger question, "Is God speaking?" If the answer is in the affirmative and is a hearty yes, then I have completed the first task of my venture into authorship.

There may be areas of doctrine, theology or biblical interpretation that you disagree with, and if you feel it is necessary I am happy to hear from you and consider your opinions and views. Please, however, consider the weight of the prophetic word. If we believe God is in this, our response should be to receive it by faith and act upon it if we are to be a part of what God wants to do among His people in these days.

PART TWO

PENTECOST THEN

A PRACTICAL, BIBLICAL LOOK AT THE WORK OF THE HOLY SPIRIT IN THE LIFE OF THE BELIEVER.

INTRODUCTION

As we move on from the prophetic consideration of "What is God saying now?" the second part of the book is intended to look at "What has God already said?"; to look afresh at the biblical record and revelation of the person and work of the Holy Spirit.

Again, I thank God for the heritage of a good foundation established through the teaching and experience of some of the early Pentecostal fathers. My lecturers at Bible College included John and Howard Carter, two brothers who were part of the founding body of the Assemblies of God movement in the UK. They had been part of the move of the Holy Spirit in the late 20's and 30's when the Holy Spirit's influence had been rampant in the ministries of Smith Wigglesworth and the Jeffreys brothers. They had shaped their understanding of the Baptism in the Holy Spirit through a lifetime of investigating and exploring the scriptures as well as their personal experiences. Their teaching, alongside others from that generation, were instrumental in my coming to an understanding of the things of the Spirit.

It was the practical application of that theology, in the ministry of Clyde and Norman Young as well as John Philips in imparting the Holy Spirit, that led me to long for this anointing. They inspired thousands of people at conferences to believe God for this experience. I understood from them the need to inspire faith in people to enter into this wonderful experience of being filled with the Spirit.

I do not pretend to be an academic nor a theologian in the accepted sense of the words, but I do aspire to be a bible teacher who accesses the truth that leads to a knowledge of God and revelation about Him. In that sense I am a student of theology; as I have studied the things of God for the whole of my adult life. I am aiming for an applied theology; a practical application of the truth; a pragmatic application of what the bible teaches about the Holy Spirit. Thank God for the academics and theologians who help and support us but my aim is to make the truth come alive in people's relationship with God. It was Jesus who said, "You shall know the truth and the truth shall set you free". *(John 8:32).* The word "*know*" used in this passage means "to be intimately acquainted with". In other words, it is as we associate with the Truth and embrace it that it works for us. We could paraphrase this verse as: "The only truth you really know is the truth that sets you free," - the truth That works practically in your life!

I hope and pray that something from the following chapters helps the reader know more clearly the truth about the Holy Spirit and leads them into a deeper relationship with this wonderful Helper.

1

THE SPIRIT IN THE BIBLE

For our first adventure into the biblical revelation of the Holy Spirit, I want to engage in a brief excursion through the Old and New Testaments, looking at the increasing revelation concerning the person and work of the Holy Spirit developed through the scriptures.

The Spirit in the Old Testament.

In the Old Testament the word used almost exclusively for Spirit is the Hebrew: *"ruach"* It means; wind, breath, or spirit. It indicates power which can be devastating in its effect. It is certainly not always just dove-like, which is a revelation that emerges in the New Testament.

There is a mystery about the Spirit. We find it much more straightforward to relate to the other persons in the Godhead, as the concept of Father and Son are relationships we are more comfortable with and more naturally understand. The Holy Spirit is not a common expression that we are familiar with in our everyday lives. One of the things that I believe is unhelpful concerning the Holy Spirit is the translation of this word in the Authorised Version, commonly known as the King James Bible. It often interprets the word "pneuma" as Holy Ghost rather than Holy Spirit. In our present world and understanding this presents an image that is not in line with the meaning of the word. He is not a ghost in the dictionary meaning of the word and I appeal to Christians everywhere to desist in the use of this archaic and antiquated word. We may understand it in the Christian world but it conveys to those outside the church something that is rather odd and a little weird and "spooky". As we shall see the Holy Spirit is a person - certainly not a ghost!

The Holy Spirit is presented to us in the first chapter of the Bible as He was involved in creation. *(Gen. 1:2, Job 33:4, Ps. 33:6, Ps. 104:29,30).* His involvement in the natural creation, the creation of mankind and even the earth itself is clearly stated.

There is also a thread throughout the Old Testament of people being empowered by the Spirit for particular and special work. This is often accompanied by the words, "The Spirit of the Lord came upon them". It indicates a violent, invading force; completely irresistible; strong in might; accomplishing through them the purpose of God.

(Jdg. 3:9,10 Othniel, Jdg. 6:34 Gideon, Jdg 13:25 Samson, Eze. 2:2 Ezekiel, 1Sam19:19,20 Saul).

There are also examples of less dramatic empowering for special practical tasks or to enable leaders to complete their calling. *(Ex.31:2-5 Bezalel, Deut.34:9 Joshua, Ps. 143:10 David).* It is important to note that in the Old Testament the Spirit empowers for a specific task and then His enabling anointing is lifted. It is noticeable in the story of Samson how that for each challenging task a separate empowering came upon him.

We also see that the purpose of the Holy Spirit is to communicate, not terrify. The Spirit is indeed power, but He is morally defined power. He never uses tricks or arbitrary displays of power; there is always purpose in His activity. There is a link between the "Spirit of the Lord" and the "Word of the Lord" *(2Sam. 23:2, Ps.33:6).* Right from the account in Genesis when God spoke and the Spirit moved there is this thread of "Word and Spirit" all through the Bible.

Prophecy was the most common form of communication as men and women were moved by the Holy Spirit to speak the word of God. *(Num. 24:2, 1Sam.10:6-13, Eze. 11:5, 1Chr. 12:18, Zech. 7:12).* There were also prophetic songs and spontaneous songs. The book of Psalms contains much prophetic, Spirit - inspired revelation. *(2Sam.23:2).*

God also communicated through dreams and visions

which appear regularly as another form of the prophetic. *(Gen. 15:1, Gen. 46:2, Eze. 1:1)*.

We conclude, then that the major work of the Holy Spirit in the Old Testament is in empowering and communicating. But while we see that in the Old Testament the Spirit was given to special people for special tasks, there is another prophetic thread that speaks of a day that is coming when the Spirit will be more widely released and poured out upon all mankind. *(Num. 11:24-29, Joel 2:28-32, Jer.31:31-34, Eze. 36:25-27)*.

The Spirit in the New Testament

There is a fuller revelation of the person and work of the Holy Spirit as we enter the New Testament and the new covenant. Here the Greek word "pneuma" is translated as wind, breath, or spirit and is used of The Spirit of God more than 250 times.

One of the clear revelations is that of the personality of the Holy Spirit. The Holy Spirit is a person simply because He possesses personality. He is not an abstract force. He has the four essential elements of personality which are life; mind; emotion and will. God, the Holy Spirit, thinks, feels, wills and lives. He is a conscious, intelligent, free and moral being.

Personal properties are ascribed to the Spirit. *(Acts 7:51, 15:28, Roms. 8:27, 1Co 12:11, Roms. 15:30, 1Co 2:10-11. Eph.4:30)*.

The scriptures describe the Spirit as being able to be resisted, know pleasure; that He has a mind with which He thinks; determines and wills; has the capacity to love; has ultimate knowledge, and can even experience grief.

Personal actions are also ascribed to the Spirit. *(Mark 13:11, Rev.2:7, Acts 5:32, Roms.8:16, Acts 13:4, 20:28, Roms.8:14, Ro 8:26, 1Co 2:13, Gal 4:6).*

He speaks, He reveals, He bears witness, He commissions and appoints, He guides, prays, teaches and cries out!

The Spirit is referred to alongside the name of other persons in the Godhead with the clear intention that He should be viewed as being just as much a person as they are. In various scriptures He is referred to in contrast to the Father and the Son and even to Satan. *(Matt. 12:26-28, 28:19, 1Cor. 12:4-6, 2Co 13:14, Eph 4:4-6).*

The language of personality is used of the Holy Spirit. He is referred to with the personal pronoun, "He" not "it". The Holy Spirit is not an abstract force or power. This is particularly revealing as it is Jesus himself who makes these statements. *(John 16:13,14)*. He is also called the "parakletos"; a person who we would call an advocate or a lawyer, not an impersonal force *(John 14:16,26, 15:26, 16:7, 1John 2:1)*. He is said to remind, teach, bear witness, guide, hear, speak, and above all, glorify Jesus. This surely confirms that the Holy Spirit is a person and not an abstract being and leads us to the conclusion that He must therefore be God.

The Bible clearly reveals the deity of the Holy Spirit. It is impossible to place Him on any level less than that of deity. A personality such as this must necessarily be divine. Names of deity are given to the Spirit. He is called Lord and God. *(2Cor.3:18, Acts 5:3,4)*. Attributes and works exclusively owned by God are ascribed to the Spirit. Omnipotence – all power; Omniscience – all knowledge; sovereignty; eternal existence, and His involvement in salvation, all indicate his divinity. *(Roms. 15:18,19, 1Cor.2:10, 1Cor.12:11, Heb. 9:14, Roms.8:2,11, Tit.3:5)*.

In the New Testament the Holy Spirit is shown to be both <u>personal</u> and <u>divine</u>. Nothing revealed in the New Testament is inconsistent with the Old Testament nor causes us to question its accuracy. This is an aspect of progressive revelation. The New Testament takes up and fills out the picture begun in the Old Testament, revealing to us, not just a God who acts in power, but a God in three persons, where the Holy Spirit is a separate, distinct, divine personality within that one Godhead. In the next chapter we will look at the relationship between the Spirit and Jesus.

2

THE SPIRIT AND JESUS

The Old Testament emphasised the empowering and communicating work of the Spirit. Jesus came to fulfill the prophetic words about Him as the Servant, King and Messiah. The Hebrew word "Messiah" is translated in the Greek language as "Christos", which means "Anointed One". He came as the "Anointed One". The word abbreviated to Christ in the English translations is not a surname but rather a description of who He is and what He does. It was prophesied that *The Spirit will rest on Him*" *(Is.11:2)*. He is Jesus, the anointed one, anointed with the Holy Spirit.

In this chapter we will look at the Spirit and Jesus. He was the first person constantly and fully filled by the Holy Spirit. This is very important and indicates the transition from Old Covenant to New Covenant.

John the Baptist was the one who came to prepare the way for the coming of the Messiah. He was told that the way he would recognise this one who was the Messiah, was that the Spirit would come on Him and remain on Him. *(John 1:32-34).* He was the first one on whom the Spirit remained and so Jesus is not just the bearer of the Spirit but also the dispenser of the Spirit; the one who will baptise others in the Spirit.

Jesus – The bearer of the Spirit.

What we mean by this is that Jesus both received the Spirit and the Spirit was powerfully present and active in His life and ministry.

This began at the Baptism of Jesus. *(Matt.3:13-17, Mark 1:9-11, Luke 3:21-22, John 1:32-34).* We understand that when an event is recorded in all four gospels it indicates the significance and importance of that event. The descent of the Spirit is in all four Gospels.

The occasion was accompanied by the voice from heaven as God the Father indicated the pleasure He takes in His Son. The parallel with prophetic scriptures from the Old Testament is also important as God affirms His Son, the servant king. *(Psalm 2:7, Is.42:1)*

Luke also makes a very important statement as he declares that following His baptism in the Holy Spirit, Jesus began His ministry. *(Luke 3:23).* He set down for us a very clear indication of the need to be filled with the Holy Spirit in order to carry out effective service. If that was the case for Jesus, how much more do we need a personal encounter with the Holy Spirit?

We then see the continuing presence of the Spirit in Jesus. We are told Jesus was "full of the Holy Spirit". *(Luke 4:1)* As you may know, Luke was a medical doctor and this is a medical term. It is used again of a man covered with leprosy. *(Luke 5:12 (NASB))*. It expresses a total and complete covering. We often say, "I am full of cold", meaning we have a bad case of or even a good dose of a virus or ailment of some kind. Jesus was completely covered with the Holy Spirit. The effect of the Holy Spirit upon Jesus was outstanding. Everything Jesus did was *"in the power of the Spirit".(Acts 10:38, Luke 4:14,18-19)* He openly declares the source of His power and authority. Consider the effect not only of His actions, but also of His words, and their response from the hearers. *(Luke 4:32,36)*. They are amazed at the authority with which He speaks. It is different from the religious leaders of their day. His words carry weight. The Holy Spirit brings a dramatic reaction to His words. Even demonic forces are dealt with as He speaks.

In His manifesto Jesus speaks clearly of the reason for the empowering of the Spirit as He outlines four aspects of the works He is empowered and authorised to do: *(Luke 4:18,19)*.

1. Preaching the gospel. The announcing of the good news.

2. Deliverance, freedom and release for captives.

Forgiveness for sin and freedom from guilt.

3. Physical healing, expressed as recovery of sight but showing that healing of the body is available as a result of the empowering of the Spirit.

4. Emotional healing; any form of oppression, whatever its source. The word bruised is used in the AV. Many people struggle with all kinds of emotional pressures. Here, we are told that as a result of the enabling of the Holy Spirit, Jesus had the power to deal with these issues.

The gospel of Luke having declared these words of Jesus, then describes the practical application of this Divine manifesto with stories of the Holy Spirit's work in the lives of the people (Luke 5:17, 6:18,19). Jesus, filled with the Holy Spirit, went around doing good as the bearer of the Holy Spirit.

Jesus - The Dispenser of the Spirit.

Jesus is also the one who dispenses the Holy Spirit. He releases and gives the Holy Spirit. The New Testament reveals Jesus as both the human brother who shares the gift of the Holy Spirit and the divine Son who confers the Holy Spirit on us.

When John the Baptist appears on the scene, he states clearly that this one who is to come will *"Baptise you with the Holy Spirit and fire"* (Matt.3:11, Mark 1:8, Luke 3:16, John 1:33). Yet again there is testimony in all four gospels.

John in his gospel uses this truth to affirm that Jesus is indeed the Son of God.

It is also Jesus' testimony about Himself. He speaks of his impending return to heaven and promises to send the Holy Spirit. *(Luke 24:49, John 7:37-39, 14:16-18, 26, 15:26, 16:7, 20:22)*. John's gospel affirms over and over the words of Jesus promising the personal and particular coming of the Holy Spirit to those who believe; the invitation to *"Come to me and drink"* being the clearest and most positive declaration of intent. John understands this as a prophetic statement speaking of the coming of the Holy Spirit, who is to be received.

The rest of the New Testament looks back to confirm that Jesus is the one who releases the promise of the Holy Spirit into the life of the believer, with references in the book of Acts and the epistles. *(Acts 2:33, 11:15-17, 1Cor.12:13, Gal.3:5,14, 4:4-6)*. The writers clearly affirm Jesus as the one who empowers men and women by baptising them with the Holy Spirit.

In conclusion, Jesus is clearly shown in the New Testament as a person filled with the Holy Spirit and therefore able to heal and set free those oppressed by the devil. As a reward for His obedience and sacrifice, He is given the Holy Spirit by the Father, who He pours out on His disciples, from heaven, on the Day of Pentecost.

The challenge to us is in the words of Jesus as He comes to the end of His ministry on earth: *"As the Father sent me.....so I send you." (John 20:21)*. Jesus calls us to aspire to receive a greater empowering of the Spirit: He proclaims that we will do *"Greater works" (John 14:12)*. than Jesus Himself.

3

THE SPIRIT AND SALVATION

The Holy Spirit is involved in the process of salvation as a person comes *"into Christ."* Paul is very clear about the work of the Spirit as a person comes to faith. *(1Cor.2:1-5)* Jesus himself was very explicit that salvation is initiated by and carried out as a result of the activity of the Holy Spirit. *(John 6:44,63, 16:7-15).*

The work of convicting and convincing men and women of their need of salvation is attributed by Jesus to the Holy Spirit. The action of taking the truth about Jesus and revealing it to mankind is again a characteristic of the work of the Spirit. He, the Holy Spirit, is involved in the process of taking us from being opposed to Christ to being included in Christ. The process of Christian initiation is shot through with references to the operation of the Spirit. The "Ordo Salutis" - the way of salvation, is the process by which the Holy Spirit applies the work of redemption in our lives.

We do not believe in selection, but we do acknowledge the truth of election according to fore-knowledge, that God sets apart those who will respond to Him and the Spirit is clearly involved in this activity. Before we believe and obey the gospel, the Holy Spirit is at work in our lives. *(John 6:44,63, 16:7-15)*. God chooses and the Spirit sets apart. So many of us, in our testimonies, recognise the way that God began His work in our lives before we ever made a personal commitment to follow Him. This was the Holy Spirit moving, working, preparing the way for us to come to faith in Christ.

It is fascinating how Paul describes the involvement of the Holy Spirit in drawing men and women to salvation. It is the Holy Spirit who moves upon the Word of God and powerfully calls people to respond. *(1 Thess.1:5)*.

Then again, the experience of regeneration; being born again, coming to spiritual life; is clearly the responsibility of the Holy Spirit. He is the one who does the work of implanting eternal life, spiritual life, into the life of the new believer. The parallels between natural birth and spiritual birth are unmistakable and undeniable. *(John 3:3-7, James 1:21, 1Pet.1:23)*. This phrase: the *"implantation of seed"*, is a reference to intercourse whereby seed is planted which brings conception. It is the Spiritual equivalent of natural conception, of being born of the Spirit. According to the letter to Titus this is all down to the Holy Spirit applying the work of Jesus to our lives. *(Tit.3:5)*. We acknowledge the importance of the activity of the Holy Spirit in every individual who comes into a relationship with God through the Lord Jesus Christ.

The Holy Spirit and assurance of Salvation.

The work of assurance refers to the activity of the Holy Spirit in each believer so that they know they are truly accepted in Christ. We are not expected merely to believe and convince ourselves that we really belong to God. Nor is it something that we should only expect to receive after many years as a believer. When we look carefully at the scriptures we see that this issue is not just an assent to a theological idea but that the Holy Spirit is looking to apply this truth and make it real in our lives. Over the years I have spent many hours with people seeking to help them come to an assurance of salvation; it is only in recent years that I have seen that it is not a matter of just words, but of people having an encounter with the Holy Spirit that causes them to see, believe and understand who they are "in Christ".

There are five words used in the New Testament for different aspects of assurance.

1. Adoption.

The Greek word "huiothesia". (Eph.1:5, Gal.4:5-6, Roms.8:15). This word is used on several occasions in the scripture and speaks of the practice of Roman adoption in the day in which Paul lived. As a Roman citizen, he would understand the full significance of adoption. Roman adoption was different to adoption in our day and included four main consequences.

1. The adopted person lost all rights to his old family and gained all the rights of a fully legitimate son in his new family.

2. It followed that they became heir to their new father's estate.

3. In law the old life of the adopted person was completely wiped out. All records were erased.

4. In the eyes of the law the adopted person was literally and absolutely the child of their new father.

The implications of this understanding needs to be applied to our "adoption" into the family of God. Our relationship with the Father and the Son is very important. It means God becomes our Father and enables us to speak with Him in intimate terms. He is our "Abba Father". This speaks of the deepest level of relationship.

Some interpret this as "Dad" or "Daddy" I prefer the full literal interpretation, "My very own dear Father". That's who God has become to us. We are totally and absolutely His children. That's why Paul uses the phrase "Joint-heirs" with Christ. It was through this adoption that we become as much a son of God as Jesus Himself. We are totally and completely the sons of Father God! This is the revelation that the Holy Spirit brings to us, which causes us to "cry out". *(Roms.8:14-17, Gal.4:6,7)*.

When we receive this revelation it impacts our emotions, it touches more than our minds; it inspires our hearts. It is *"by the Spirit"* that we are able to acknowledge God as Abba. This will bring security and a sense of well- being to us as we allow the Holy Spirit to work this truth into our lives.

2. "Seal"

Seal is the second word used. It speaks of evidence of ownership. The Greek word "sphragizo" means "to seal". It shows who you belong to. One of reasons speaking in tongues is important is that it shows that we have been "sealed". It is a further proof that we are in Christ. The truth is spoken in 3 different ways and suggests we have been anointed, sealed and that a deposit securing us has been paid. *(2Cor.1:21-22, Eph.1:13, 4:30)*.

3. "Deposit".

The next word is deposit, pledge or down payment. The Greek word "arrabon" means all of these. It is a financial word describing how we secure a purchase by paying a deposit. It is declaring the Holy Spirit to be the assurance that because the down payment has been made, we can be assured that the final payment will follow. *(Eph.1:14, 2Cor.1:22, 2Cor.5:5)* There is absolutely no doubt that all the promises and provision of God for completing our salvation will take place. It is not without significance that in modern Greek the word "arrabon" is used for engagement ring. How appropriate that is for us with the biblical revelation that we are the bride of Christ. He is engaged to us with the guarantee that we will become His bride. This brings us assurance.

4. "Firstfruits".

Word four is a farming analogy. The word "firstfruits", the Greek "aparche", indicates an expectation that if the firstfruits are good, the rest of the crop will be. The Holy Spirit is given as the firstfruits of the harvest God has in store for us. *(Roms. 8:23)* We are assured by the Spirit of His good intentions to give us a full inheritance.

5. "Assurance".

The final word used is the word assurance itself, in some translations the word used is conviction. *(1Thess.1:5)*. The Greek word is "plerophoria" and it means full assurance, entire confidence; it literally means "full carrying". This is not merely an intellectual persuasion but an overwhelming convincing. We are totally assured of our relationship with God. There is no doubt about it.

When Jesus was baptized, heaven opened and the Father spoke of His pleasure in His Son. *(Luke 3:21-23)*. I believe that God by His Spirit wants us to know that He loves us and is proud of us and we can be assured that /He will never let us down.

It is important that we acknowledge the important work of the Holy Spirit in Salvation.

4

THE BAPTISM OF THE HOLY SPIRIT

There is an experience known as the baptism with the Holy Spirit. The Bible uses the term to define a distinct personal encounter with the person of the Holy Spirit. We have already seen how that Jesus Himself was filled with the Holy Spirit. It is interesting to note that John the Baptist testified that Jesus would baptise people with the Holy Spirit and with fire; Jesus prophesied that people would receive the Holy Spirit as they came to Him and believed on Him and Peter on the day of Pentecost declared that Jesus had filled them with the Holy Spirit. (*Matt.3:11, John 7:37-39, Acts 2:16-33*). What John had declared and Jesus prophesied, happened on that momentous day.

The remarkable conclusion of Peter's message on the Day of Pentecost was that this experience of being filled with the Holy Spirit was for every believer. It was not just for Jesus or the early Apostles. It was and is for you and me, for every future generation. We can receive the Holy Spirit. *(Acts 2:38,39)*.

When Peter answered the question from the crowd he spoke of the process of fully coming into a relationship with God, as he spoke of repentance and faith, baptism in water and then receiving the gift of the Holy Spirit. David Pawson, in his excellent book, "The Normal Christian Life", describes this as Christian Initiation. The early Pentecostals spoke of "Full salvation"; that God's purpose for every believer was this threefold initiation into Christ. There is a large Pentecostal denomination in the USA called the "Foursquare movement". It is based upon the four pillars of Jesus as the Saviour, Baptiser in the Holy Spirit, Healer and Coming King. It is suggested that being baptised in the Holy Spirit is an essential element of our relationship with God. It is not an optional extra for those who are in ministry or especially keen to be used by God. It is a fundamental necessity for every believer in order to live in the way God intends.

Distinct from Salvation.

Although very much part of salvation, it is distinct from the experience of repentance and faith; although as we shall see there are examples of people being baptised with the Holy Spirit at the same time they received Christ as Saviour and Lord.

People are often confused by the different terms used. "Baptism in the Holy Spirit", "being filled with the Spirit" or "receiving the Holy Spirit." Any examination of the scriptures must lead to the conclusion that these are synonymous terms describing the same encounter and experience with the Spirit. *(Matt.3:11, John 7:37-39, Acts. 2:4)*. The way these verses describe the same event as they overlap is clear as you read them.

There have also been some unnecessary and unhelpful comments about whether it is "Baptism in, with or by the Spirit." The answer is simple the Greek word "en" can be any of the three so all of those terms are acceptable.

As to the distinctive nature of the Baptism with the Spirit, the teaching of Jesus is clear. He addresses His disciples in the discourse in John's gospel and makes it clear that the Spirit who is "with you shall be in you" *(John 14:16,17)*. It is clear they knew His presence but were not "filled" with the Spirit. They were saved, had experienced forgiveness, (Jesus proclaimed, *"you are already clean"* *(John 15:3)* but they were to wait to receive an empowering of the Spirit. Luke is very clear on the order as he concludes the gospel of Luke with the disciples waiting for the Holy Spirit and introduces the book of Acts with them receiving the Holy Spirit. *(Luke 24:49, Acts 2:1-4)*

In the teaching of Jesus in John chapters 14-16, the emphasis is that they needed the Holy Spirit to take the place of Jesus in order to continue the work. There is a fascinating use of words to explain that the Holy Spirit was to come to reproduce the same effect in them as they had known while Jesus was with them. There are two words for "another" in the Greek language. One means "another but of a different kind" the other, used here in John's gospel means "another of exactly the same kind" This is the word, "allos" *(John 14:16).* It can be illustrated in a number of ways, but means for us that being filled with the Spirit is essentially the same for us as if Jesus was present. The Holy Spirit is another of exactly the same kind. That means for us, we experience His presence with and in us.

There are many biblical pictures, patterns and teaching that enable us to see our need for a distinct and clear Baptism in the Holy Spirit.

There is the Old Testament shadow or type. We see in the Old Testament that when God called men and women, he equipped them for the task. Gideon would be one example among many. *(Judges 6:34)* There are also many types and symbols of the Spirit: Aaron was anointed with oil; Elijah had his mantle or coat; Moses his rod; David was anointed with oil to be King. All these are shadows of what was to come and which find their ultimate fulfilment in the empowering of the Holy Spirit *(Hebs.10:1).* They were the people of God who for service and ministry required the "filling of the Spirit".

Even the Lord Jesus, before He commenced His public ministry received the Spirit. Consider the graphic description of the Spirit descending upon Jesus in the form of a dove, emphasising His personal empowering for ministry. The statement *"Jesus began His ministry"* follows His Baptism and receiving of the Spirit. *(Luke 3:21-23)* With all the legends and myths surrounding the development of Jesus ministry there were no miracles or ministry before his Baptism in the Spirit. If Jesus needed to be "filled with the Spirit" to commence and carry out His ministry, how much more do we!

Then we have the references in the book of Acts to people being filled with the Holy Spirit: the Disciples of Jesus, the one hundred and twenty gathered in the upper room; *(Acts 2:1-4)* the testimony of the early Church in Samaria and Ephesus and also Paul's own personal experience, all clearly defined experiences of receiving the Holy Spirit. *(Acts 8:12,17. 19:2,6. 9:17)*.

It is important to note that this is not a prescriptive order. It almost feels as though the Holy Spirit inspires Luke to write of people coming to "full salvation" in different circumstances and order to save us from "organising" the way He works and moves. It is clear from the experience in the house of Cornelius that the Holy Spirit fell upon them as they were listening to Peter preaching. They had not been "baptised in water" and we do not read they "came to the front", or "put their hand up", or "prayed the sinner's prayer", but they clearly opened up to God. I would suggest that their salvation and baptism with the Spirit were simultaneous. *(Acts 10:44-47)*. I know of this occurring even in our day. At our Bible College we had an Italian student from Milan. His name was Pasquale

Barcelona. He had been brought up as a Catholic but did not know the Lord. He attended a Pentecostal Church for the first time, heard the gospel preached and was responding in his heart to the message. As the preacher came to a conclusion and was about to appeal, my friend felt a welling up from within and an urgency to speak. He began to speak with other languages he had never heard. He knew nothing about being filled with the Holy Spirit or speaking in tongues. As he was responding to the message of salvation, he was filled with the Holy Spirit. God is sovereign and He sometimes surprises us.

Paul's teaching defines this distinction by the use of the words "after you believed" *(Eph.1:13, 2Cor.1:21,22).* The fact that following their believing they received the Spirit is clearly intended by Paul.

Before the outpouring of the Holy Spirit in the early 20th century which gave rise to the Pentecostal movement of churches, there are various testimonies from Church history which speak of this baptism of the Spirit. The early church fathers testify to the receiving of the Spirit. Heroes from the past give testimony to an experience of receiving the Spirit, particularly graphic are those of Charles Finney and D.L. Moody. R.A. Torrey wrote a book on this subject at the end of the 19th century. The worldwide outpouring that continues to this day testifies to this truth.

We acknowledge that there are a number of opinions about this truth. The view called cessationism was the traditional evangelical view: that salvation and the baptism in the Spirit were synonymous; that the gifts of the Spirit ceased when the Bible was completed. They were no longer necessary. There is another view called procession, popularly known as Third Wave. This suggests the Spirit is received at salvation but requires activating! I believe this is confusing and an attempt to compromise. However, even if this theory is believed, it underlines the necessity of a distinct encounter with the Holy Spirit. Imt is my submission that the traditional Pentecostal and Charismatic view of the Baptism in the Holy Spirit is the correct understanding of scriptures. It is a distinct experience. In the next chapter we will look at further truth concerning being filled with the Holy Spirit.

5

BEING FILLED WITH THE HOLY SPIRIT

In this chapter we want to look at the practical issues surrounding the Baptism of the Spirit. There are valid questions that need to be answered. Who should be filled with the Holy Spirit? Why should I be filled with the Spirit? Do I qualify to be filled with the Holy Spirit? What difference will it make and how can I know I am filled with the Spirit? I submit below some suggestions which I hope will go some way in helping us to a greater understanding of the Baptism in the Spirit.

This experience is for every believer.

No one is excluded or unqualified. The prophet Joel wrote this experience is for "all flesh" *(Joel 2:28),* which means every human being on the planet regardless of age, colour, education or race. The term all flesh is fully inclusive. Peter on the day of Pentecost went to great lengths to ensure that we understood this was not just for the listening audience hearing him speak but for every future generation as well. *(Acts 2:38,39)*. The very clear intention of Peter is to make it clear that even to this day the Holy Spirit is for *"all that the Lord our God shall call"* - every believer in Jesus.

The emphasis of the words of Jesus in John chapters 14-16 are very important. *"I am going away"*, *"You can do nothing without me"*. I can imagine the despair in the disciples and a cry of "Help, how are we going to survive?" He then reassures them *"I will send the Holy Spirit to take my place"*."He will be to you all that I have been". Remember the "another" from the last chapter. He, the Holy Spirit will be exactly as I have been to you. He actually says it is necessary for Him to go away to enable the Holy Spirit to come and empower more than His immediate followers. Jesus could only directly influence the people of His day while in His humanity. He could not influence the future, as He was returning to heaven following His death and resurrection. *(John 16:7 AV)* Future influence would be by the Holy Spirit, directly from heaven or by special revelation.

It is not dependent upon qualification

Peter was very clear that the Holy Spirit was a "gift". *(Acts 2:38)*. That means it cannot be earned or deserved and is not dependent upon reaching a certain level of competence, holiness or biblical knowledge. The word gift is "Charismata", a word bringing together two Greek words: "Charis" which means grace and "mata" which means gift. It is therefore a grace gift, completely undeserved and unearned.

It is very important to realise that the Baptism in the Holy Spirit is not an optional extra. When you buy a vehicle you are given the option of adding extras that the manufacturer suggests will make the whole car experience a better one, but you must pay for those additions. The Baptism with the Spirit is not like that. It is not an option, but rather like the engine of the car, it is an essential part of the believer's life. Peter emphasises this is for you! Not a select few. Jesus said you cannot manage without the Baptism of the Holy Spirit. Why try? The Baptism of Holy Spirit is given by God as a Divine act of kindness and favour!

Receiving the Spirit is dependent upon desire.

The real question is "Do you want to be filled with the Spirit?" Desire is at the heart of every spiritual encounter and experience with God. Jesus put it very simply in terms of thirst. *(John 7:37-39)*. If you are thirsty you need a drink to quench your thirst. The invitation of Jesus was then and still is, *"Come and drink"*. John is absolutely clear that Jesus was referring to the Holy Spirit who was to come, and who did come on the day of Pentecost. This is the only qualifying factor. You do not have to have attained some level of spirituality or been through some course or class but simply to have a longing to be filled with the Spirit.

I have also regularly come across people who have a fear of being baptised in the Spirit. They know they should be, but have been put off because they have seen very weird and wonderful things said and done in the name of the Holy Spirit. I remember my first visit to Jamaica and some of the small Pentecostal groups in the rural areas. A number of women, usually older, would get very excited and scream and shake and generally act out of control. I noticed that none of the young people had any interest in being filled with the Spirit. One sensed that they observed that if this was what it meant to receive the Spirit they would rather not! I do remember as a young man being wary of a couple of people in our church circle who, when believing the Holy Spirit was wanting to manifest, would begin to warm up like a steam train. Huffing and puffing and gradually warming up until they would burst out in tongues at a decibel level that shook the building! I do not believe that is necessary or helpful. Jesus was clear that if we desire to be filled with the Spirit, *"It is a good thing we desire". (Luke 11:11-13).* There is nothing harmful or frightening about being filled with the Spirit. God only wants to give us good things! For many of us when we were filled with the Holy Spirit, it was a dramatic experience but not an uncontrolled display of emotion.

We receive the Spirit by faith.

One of the things I learnt from those early Pentecostal leaders that God used to impart the Holy Spirit, usually through the laying on of hands, was the importance of encouraging and inspiring faith. As believers we know that everything we receive from God we receive by faith. *(Heb.11:6)*. The scripture is clear, we cannot please God and therefore receive anything from God without faith. Bill Johnson in his excellent book "God is Good" suggests that "what we believe about God will have an effect on our lives in a measurable way because he rewards those who have set their hearts on discovering Him"[2]. A conviction that God wants to fill us with the Holy Spirit is essential. Jesus really does mean that if we are thirsty He will fill us with His Holy Spirit.

Paul takes the matter a little further when he announces in several verses in Galatians that we receive the promise of the Spirit by faith *(Gal.3:2,14)*. The Baptism of the Holy Spirit is to be actively pursued and sought. The language of the apostles in the book of Acts was for people to receive and not to hold back and wait. There seems to be a misconception that is expressed in statements such as "If God wants to fill me with the Holy Spirit He can", or even misguided counsel "to wait". The only time waiting was encouraged was BEFORE the Holy Spirit was poured out on the day of Pentecost. *(Luke 24:49)*. Since He came on that great day there is no need to wait but rather receive! Many thousands around the world are still being filled with the Holy Spirit as they reach out in faith with a longing for Him to come.

---

[2] God is Good – He's better than you think – Bill Johnson. P85.

Practical steps to receiving the Spirit.

Having been around for so many years I have seen the extremes of people pressing, shaking, shouting and altogether being over enthusiastic in encouraging people to be filled with the Spirit. Often this is related to speaking in tongues and can lead to very unhealthy practices, the most common of which is to encourage people to make up words! The proverbial, "Say banana backwards" was a standing joke in some circles.

I have also come across the opposite which is so passive: that to be filled with the Spirit does not mean anything and people are not encouraged to expect anything. I remember a conversation with a solicitor who had been to a large Christian event where they were encouraged to be filled with the Spirit and they were told they would know that they had received the Spirit because they would do something they never usually did. He went back to his chalet and cleaned his shoes, suggesting this was evidence that he had been filled with the Spirit. He assured me his wife usually completed this task on his behalf. I am equally unhappy with such a weak approach this has no biblical foundation.

I do believe we should aspire to be filled with the Spirit and receive by faith the Baptism of the Holy Spirit, expecting an encounter with God that is radical, positive and life-changing. Every time someone was filled with the Holy Spirit in the Bible, there was a physical and spiritual reaction and response which resulted in significant change.

Of course we have to face the issues of tongues. There is no doubt that tongues, or languages, is a sign of the coming of the Spirit, ONE of the signs. *(Acts 2:1-4, 10:44-47, 19:6).* Tongues was clearly accepted as evidence of Holy Spirit Baptism. It is very clear that Peter uses the example of Cornelius and his friends speaking with tongues as proof of their encounter with the Spirit.

In the other two examples of people receiving the Spirit in the book of Acts, although tongues is not mentioned there is an inference of some physical response as they were filled with the Spirit. In the Samaritan account Simon "SAW" something that gave rise to his request to purchase the ability to impart the Spirit - a physical evidence. *(Acts 8:17,18)*

The other account of someone being filled with the Spirit concerns Paul. There is no mention of tongues at that time but subsequently it is Paul who is the great champion in encouraging others to speak with other tongues as he declares, *"I speak in tongues more that all of you"* and *"I would that you all spoke in tongues" (Acts 9:17, 1Cor.14:5,18).*

A couple of observations here. I am intrigued by the translators use of the word "tongues". Most versions of the Bible interpret the Greek word "glossolalia" in that way. However, in our common use of the word we would say "languages" rather than tongues. It is the same word. I think sometimes the word tongues is seen as a little weird and off the track, carrying a kind of odd nuance. I wonder if the translators had simply said languages, whether that would be a help to some who immediately think of some ecstatic jabbering.

I am also suggesting that all those who receive the Holy Spirit have the capacity to speak in tongues. There are some Pentecostal movements who state that tongues is the initial evidence that someone has received the Spirit. I understand that but struggle to align myself with that stance. Clearly many people are baptised in the Spirit and do not speak with tongues. They express all the qualities of a spirit filled life but openly state that they have not and do not speak in tongues. I do believe that all those who have encountered the Spirit have the capacity to speak with other tongues and their experience with God would be enhanced by this wonderful ability to speak with other languages. Paul makes the statement that through the language of the Spirit believers can build themselves up; why would God give that ability to some and not others? *(1Cor.14:4)*.

I believe faith is the key. When I lay hands on people to receive the Holy Spirit I encourage them to believe God. As He comes upon them and they sense the "living water flowing from their innermost being" *(John 7:38)*, they should speak in faith expecting their mouths to be filled with languages they have never learnt. For me this follows the pattern on the day of Pentecost; as they are filled with the Spirit they began to speak and as they speak God fills their mouths with new languages. *(Acts 2:1-4)*.

I do believe there are other marks and indications that someone is filled with the Holy Spirit. To suggest Billy Graham or the late Martin Lloyd Jones are not Spirit-filled men because they do not testify to speaking in tongues is unwise and unhelpful. There are other evidences of a Spirit filled life. We will look at this in the next chapter and also explain a little more about the various aspects of speaking in the language of the Spirit.

However, this does not undermine the importance of tongues related to the Holy Spirit. Many Christians are not baptised by immersion in water! That does not invalidate the importance of water baptism. Let us be people filled with all God has for us, open for a powerful, transforming encounter with the Person of the Holy Spirit that includes speaking in languages we have never learnt.

6
THE IMPACT OF THE BAPTISM IN THE HOLY SPIRIT

The Baptism with the Holy Spirit has a major impact in a believer's life. There are other evidences besides tongues that mark a person out as being filled with the Spirit. The Baptism in the Spirit intensifies and makes more real every spiritual activity. Being filled with the Spirit deepens and increases every spiritual dynamic. Many years ago when there was a particular move of the Holy Spirit, the question was asked of Bob Gordon, a great Scottish bible teacher in the Charismatic tradition, how we could discern a genuine move of the Spirit. His answer made such an impression on me that I made note of it and have used it many times and so include it here. He suggested there were at least three genuine marks which must accompany a work of the Holy Spirit that results in:

1. A closer relationship with Jesus.

2. A deeper maturity in Christian walk.

3. A greater effectiveness in service. (fruitfulness)

I suggest at least eight areas where the Holy Spirit makes a difference.

1. New appreciation of Jesus.

When I was baptised in the Holy Spirit as a teenager there was a dramatic change in the level of my intimacy with God. As a young boy I had made a decision to give my life to Christ. That moment was very real and some 60 years on is still very much alive in my memory. However, although I knew Jesus had saved me, I had no concept of a living relationship with Him until I was baptised in the Holy Spirit. I remember the day I was filled with the Spirit and began to speak with other languages. I left the room and came out into the open air. I remember a sense of the presence of Jesus such as I had not known as if He was right there next to me. I knew He was my Saviour but as a result of the Holy Spirit He came near. I understood what Jesus meant when He said the Holy Spirit would make Jesus real, He would glorify Jesus and reveal Him to us. A major result of being filled with the Spirit is an increased capacity for worship, and ability to express our love and appreciation for Him. *(John 16:14,15)* This has to do with relationship. A deepening awareness of His presence. His major activity is to glorify Jesus.

2. New appreciation of the Bible.

The Holy Spirit is the author of the Bible and therefore the best interpreter. When the Holy Spirit fills us, many testify to a new love and regard for the Bible, not as a textbook but as a living word. God speaks to them as they read and meditate. The scriptures come alive in a new and powerful way. There is a very significant testimony in the biography of Smith Wigglesworth. He was a simple Bradford plumber, not educated but hungry for God. He went to Sunderland and came back filled with the Holy Spirit. The next Sunday he stood to preach the Word of God. There was such revelation and fluency as he spoke that his wife called out in the meeting, "That's not my Smith". The Holy Spirit had brought the Bible alive in such a wonderful way that his wife recognised something significant had resulted when he was filled with the Holy Spirit. Again there is testimony about this remarkable man that wherever he was, whoever he was with, following lunch he would excuse himself and go into a room alone with his Bible and read for at least one hour every day. This is evidence of the reality of the work of the Spirit. *(2Pet.1:21, John 14:26, 16:13).*

3. New authority in witness

Jesus himself was very direct with those early disciples as he was about to leave the earth for heaven. He encouraged them to receive the Holy Spirit and indicated that power would accompany that experience. *(Acts 1:8).* He used the Greek word "dunamis" from which we have derived our word dynamite. This was to be explosive power. It was clear that the purpose of the power was not for a self-indulgent display of tricks but for the purpose of others becoming believers in Jesus. This is a primary purpose for us to be filled with the Holy Spirit.

I am delighted that at this present time the church seems to be waking up to this essential and vital truth. It is important to notice He does not give the ability to witness but rather authority in witnessing. Note the words "that ye might BE witnesses", not "DO witnessing", not winning arguments but seeing the power of the Spirit work through us. In recent days many believers in our area have been on the streets and had the joy of seeing people respond to a simple presentation of the good news about Jesus. When we lose this focus we lose our reason for being.

4. New activity in praise.

When we receive the Holy Spirit we receive this wonderful capacity to worship using the ability to speak in tongues. (Please note there are at least six aspects of speaking in tongues outlined below). The use of our own language is so limited we find ourselves without the competence to express the deep feelings of emotion and affection we feel towards the Lord Jesus. In the context of worship, our language resources are soon exhausted. The language of the Spirit takes us into another dimension. Paul discovered the wonderful blessing of worshipping the Lord in other languages as the Spirit enabled him. *(1 Cor.14:15, Eph.5:18,19)*. So often we come to the end of ourselves and by the Spirit soar to new heights of presence, worship and release as we use this gift that has been given to us. I cannot count the number of times as I have been in the context of worship that a release of speaking with tongues has carried us into a new dimension of the Lord's presence. I am sure it is the intention of God that every believer should enjoy this privilege.

5. New attitude in prayer.

Tongues are also part of our prayer life which we are encouraged to see as part of our prayer activity. *(1Co 14:14,15)*. When you do not know how to pray, you release the burden by the Spirit praying through you as you pray in tongues. Your mind and understanding is so overwhelmed by the burden you carry that through the Spirit as you speak with other languages you release the weight of what you feel to God. Your mind is unfruitful but your spirit prays. In these days when so often we do not know how to pray for the situations in which we find ourselves, particularly with regard to world affairs. I believe we should spend much time using the language of the Spirit.

Over the years I have experienced some special occasions when tongues have been a powerful means of prayer. We were praying on a Sunday evening gathering in a church in Essex. That morning a lady had turned up at the meeting quite distressed and in trouble. My wife and one of the elders had counselled her and encouraged her to commit her way and life to Jesus. The lady had gone away but the elder had left his address with her. At this prayer gathering we were encouraged to pray for her. As we sought the Lord together I began to feel a stirring within and began to pray in tongues. I was aware the volume began to increase until I was speaking quite strongly. After several minutes the feeling subsided and I quietened down and the prayer meeting continued. After the gathering one of the young men came to me and said, "Do you speak German?" I replied that I had never completed any studies in the German language. He then advised me that I was speaking perfect sentences in this tongue and calling this lady to surrender to God and give her life to the Lord. At 11pm that evening the elder was surprised by a knock on his door as this lady arrived in floods of tears requesting that he pray with her.

In the book "With signs following" by Stanley Frodsham written about the outpouring of the Spirit at the beginning of the 20th century, the author gives many examples of the use of tongues in prayer using existing languages. I do believe we have neglected to practise this aspect of prayer and thereby undervalued a wonderful resource of intercession. I believe the Spirit is encouraging us to develop and grow in it.

6. New atmosphere of living

This word *edification* means to build up. *(1Cor.14:4)*. The thought here is of a spiritual exercise: putting on spiritual muscle, as a means of building up the believer; as a means of strength; as an answer to depression; as a means of encouraging spiritual sensitivity; as the means of being constantly filled with the Spirit, every day. *(Eph 5:18,19)*.

I thank God that when I was filled with the Holy Spirit as a young man, I was given such wise and practical advice. We were encouraged to exercise this ability to speak with tongues every day. Over the years when I have been struggling and feeling down I have used this wonderful facility to press through and break through. I remember as a young pastor coming home after a particularly difficult meeting with a particularly difficult person feeling quite drained and exhausted. I felt I should go to my room and kneel before the Lord and speak in tongues. As I knelt before the Lord using this wonderful gift from God I found the heaviness lifting and the Lord strengthening me. I advocate this for all believers who are filled with the Holy Spirit. Living from the inside out, from the Spirit, He imposes His presence upon the soul and the body and lifts us out of our depression.

It is interesting that Paul, who speaks of prolific speaking with tongues, also speaks of being content in every situation. *(1Cor.14:18, Phil. 4:11).*

An interesting aside…How did he know he spoke with tongues more than anybody else? I can only assume he spoke in tongues so much that he knew nobody could speak in tongues more!

7. New aspiration in ministry

As a result of being filled with the Holy Spirit we are given entrance into the supernatural workings of God. By the gifts of the Holy Spirit, we are equipped for ministry and have access into new spheres of service *(Lk 4:18, 1Co 12:7- 9)*. These 9 gifts outlined by Paul are seen in the life and ministry of Jesus. Apart from Tongues and Interpretation the gospels are full of examples of these gifts. They are important and necessary for us in fulfilling the mandate that we have been given. Further study is essential and another book will cover this subject.

8. New access to holiness.

If we are truly filled with the Holy Spirit we must be led into holy living. He is the HOLY Spirit. He leads into holy living. A heightened conscience is the result of the work of the Spirit in us. I am not impressed by someone who claims to be filled with the Spirit but does not show signs of godly living. The scripture is quite clear *(Gal 5:16-18, Ro 8:14-17 N.B. 12,13)*. These verses are quite clear about the Holy Spirit leading us into clean and righteous living. Somebody said, "You cannot commit adultery and speak in tongues at the same time". That's quite brutal and straight but it is the truth.

Notes on Tongues and the Holy Spirit.

I believe it is God's purpose for every believer to speak with tongues. *(1Co 14:5,18)*. Paul experienced the value and knew the blessing of tongues-speaking. Spiritual muscle, sensitivity and blessing result from this exercise. Does God have favourites who are to know this blessing and others who cannot or do not? The answer is NO! It is important to realise Paul was correcting excess in Corinth, not speaking against the use of tongues. If Paul was writing to the church today he might be saying, *"Can we have a few more tongues"?* not restricting their use to 2 or 3. The church in Corinth were obviously experiencing an excessive use of the gifts of the Spirit. *(1Cor.14:26).* He was equally clear that abuse was not an excuse for no use! I know of churches where public use of tongues is frowned upon! *(1Co 14:39 "do not forbid to speak with tongues").*

One of the reasons confusion has arisen is because of a lack of understanding that there are different expressions and uses for speaking in tongues. As I understand the scriptures I can find at least 6 different reasons for speaking in tongues. In interpreting the passages in Corinthians it is important to ascertain which of those particular uses Paul is referring to.

1. As an evidence of the Baptism of the Spirit.

It is important to distinguish between the personal and devotional use of tongues which comes as the result of being baptised in the Spirit and the public gift of the Spirit. Confusion has arisen because of the suggestion that all do not speak in tongues. *(1Co 12:30).* It is important to note the context of this passage. It is clear that this is to do with the church functioning in ministry and different gifts being expressed. This is not referring to the private and devotional use of tongues, but the public Gift of Holy Spirit in church gatherings. *(1Co 12:10).* This is usually accompanied by an interpretation. *(1Cor.14:26,27).* This is the gift of tongues. The ability to speak in tongues comes as a result of the Gift of the Holy Spirit. I believe that distinction is helpful in understanding this subject.

2. As a Gift of the Holy Spirit.

I believe that is clear from the above. I know of many Spirit filled believers who speak in tongues with great freedom and liberty who have never publically been used by God in giving what has become known as a message in tongues. I know for myself I have enjoyed a freedom in the prophetic realm but only once as a young man felt constrained to bring a tongue in a church gathering.

3. As a praise language.

In the context of worship, our language resources are soon exhausted. The language of the Spirit takes us into another dimension. *(1Co 14:15, Eph 5:18,19.)*

4. As a prayer language.

We have already covered this earlier in the chapter.

5. As a means of building ourselves up.

As we have seen.

6. As a means of evangelism.

It is clear that on the day of Pentecost it was the supernatural event of the believers speaking with tongues that arrested the attention of the crowd and provided the environment for Peter to preach his great sermon. *(Acts 2:7-*

12). I realise there are some difficulties with interpreting some aspects of Paul's teaching on this matter in 1 Cor.14. However, whatever he means, it is clear that tongues is an effective means to open people up to the gospel and prepare them for God to speak. I recently read a theological treatise looking at tongues with regard to unbelievers. Serious theologians were disagreeing about what a certain Greek word might mean in 1 Corinthians 14. As I read, I was reminded of the Day of Pentecost and understood that whatever Paul's intended meaning, he was correcting excess and not forbidding speaking with other tongues either in the public place or in church gatherings. I will develop this further in the next book on the Gifts of the Holy Spirit.

My prayer in this chapter is not that you agree with all my findings but that it opens your heart and mind to further understand and explore what it means to be filled with the Holy Spirit.

Every believer can... and should by faith *(Mk 16:16)*. The question is not "Do I need to speak in tongues?" but, "I need to because I want to receive all that God has for me!"

7

CONTINUALLY BEING FILLED
WITH THE SPIRIT

One of my concerns with regard to the Baptism with the Spirit is hearing people give their testimonies and referring to a date in the past when they were initially filled with the Spirit. It is almost a kind of status issue. It is as if they have sorted that one out so let us move on. I think the Bible is clear that being filled with the Spirit is an on-going issue and that we need to continually be encountering and being filled afresh with the Spirit.

Crisis/Process

Several years ago I felt the Lord showed me something that was relevant to both our natural and spiritual lives. He suggested that everything starts with a crisis and works out by a process. There is an encounter event that leads to us working out of that encounter. It is true for our natural life. It started with a crisis, at least for our mother and since then we have been working out the process of living. Around the age of 5 we commenced our education. I remember the crisis well as I cried as they separated me from my parents. We then worked out our education over a number of years. The next crisis was our vocation, and then until retirement we worked out the process. Marriage was a major crisis, a good one for many of us; we have then been working out the process. Children come, retirement comes and eventually our final crisis – death, followed by the process of working out eternity! This is not only true for our natural lives but every spiritual activity starts with crisis experience and works out by a process.

Salvation. - Our initial encounter with God. *(John 3:3-7,5:24)* We then work out our salvation. *(Phil. 2:12).*

Baptism. - This initial crisis of sanctification. *(Ro 6:6).* Worked out by the process of on-going sanctification. *(Eph 4:24)* We put off the old life and then work it out in our lives.

The Baptism in the Spirit. - There is the initial Baptism which is the crisis and then the on-going filling with the Spirit which is the process. We see this in the early church. The same disciples who are baptised with the Holy Spirit on the day of Pentecost are filled again with the Spirit during a prayer gathering *(Ac 2:1-5, 4:31)*. Peter, who again was present at Pentecost, experiences a fresh encounter with the Spirit as he addresses the crowd *(Ac 2:1-5; 4:8)*. In the NASB Reference Bible it suggests this could equally be interpreted, *"having just been filled with the Spirit"*, suggesting a special anointing at a specific time for a specific task. The same is said of Paul. *(Ac 9:17; 13:9)*. Again there is a marginal reference giving the present experience as God uses Paul in the miraculous. It is present in Paul's teaching. The same believers filled with the Spirit in Acts chapter 19 are encouraged to *"be being filled with the Spirit"*. The present continuous tense is used here. They are to continually go on being filled. *(Ac 19:1-6, Eph 5:18,19)*. It is also clear in the teaching of Jesus. *(John 7:37-39)*. The word "innermost being" means literally "womb". This is difficult when referring to men. It applies to the deepest recesses of a person, the spirit of a man touched by the Spirit of God. Again these verses are in the present continuous tense. Jesus is emphasising the importance of drinking and going on drinking, of believing and going on believing.

The encouragement here is that having started in faith we should go on living in faith. We receive by faith and continue to live by faith.

The challenge here is not, whether you were filled with the Spirit on some date in the past, but whether you are filled with the Spirit NOW!!!

8

PURPOSE – TO THE ENDS OF THE EARTH

In this last chapter I want to end with a final challenge to "keep the main thing the main thing". The purpose of the outpouring of the Holy Spirit was and still is that the nations of the earth will hear the wonderful story of salvation in and through Jesus. Right from the beginning of the story of the work of the Holy Spirit, Jesus Himself emphasised that He came upon them that they might be witnesses to the ends of the earth. *(Acts 1:8)*. The book of Acts is the story of the fulfilment of this verse as the gospel filled Jerusalem, then Samaria, then Judea and then the known world. *(Acts 17:6)* We make three brief statements.

1. The Spirit motivates evangelism.

It was Peter's testimony that we "cannot help speaking" (Acts 4:20). I worked for several years in my early ministry with an older man. He spoke of an outpouring of the Spirit upon a church he was leading which resulted in tremendous joy, dancing and extravagant worship, but he made the point that people were also motivated to share the gospel. Without prompting, or a programme being organized, they would share the gospel on trains and buses, never being without literature which they used as a point of contact.

2. The Spirit directs evangelism.

The Holy Spirit directed Philip by word and action, including this dramatic miracle of being transported! *(Acts 8:26:29,39)*. Peter testifies to being led by the Spirit. *(Acts 11:12)*. The church in Antioch are directed by the Spirit, *(Acts 13:1)* and Paul testifies to this work of the Spirit in directing him in outreach. *(Ac 16:6-7)*. The life of Jesus is saturated with Divine appointments to share the gospel indicating that he himself was "led by the Spirit". Expressed by Jesus as *"only doing the things He saw the Father doing" John 5:19)*.

3. The Spirit confirms evangelism with miraculous signs and wonders.

This wonderful expression of the Holy Spirit working in the lives of His disciples resulted in a powerful expression of the supernatural life of God, as men and women filled with the Holy Spirit saw the power of God manifested in the lives of others. (Mk 16:15,20) " *the Lord worked with them and confirmed his word by the signs that followed*".

Our prayer is, "Lord, do it again in our day and our generation. Pour out your Spirit."

ABOUT THE AUTHOR

Peter Butt trained in the Assemblies of God Bible College. Since 1970 he has been involved in church leadership. He founded and established the School of Ministries leadership training programme out of New Community Church, Southampton. He travels widely nationally and internationally training leaders as well as overseeing churches in the UK. He is married to Irene and has four married children, seven grandchildren and one great grandchild.

Peter is currently working on further books in this series with the next book due in Autumn 2018 with a working title of *"Pentecost Expressed – A Fresh Look at the Gifts of The Holy Spirit"*

If you would like a FREE preview of this book, or are interested in keeping up to date with Peter Butt's new book releases, simply head on over to www.jascottpublications.com/peterbutt and find out more.

17361000R00077

Printed in Great Britain
by Amazon